DOVER CORPORATION
50 YEARS OF ENTREPRENEURSHIP

RUSS BANHAM

FOREWORD BY RAM CHARAN

FENWICK

© 2005 by Dover Corporation

Dover Corporation
280 Park Avenue
New York, New York 10017

www.dovercorporation.com

All imagery from the collections of Dover Corporation and its businesses and used by permission of Dover Corporation, except for pages 2–3, 12–13, 66, 72–73, 92, and 112, © 2005 Ferorelli; page 12, courtesy Charan Associates, Inc.; pages 16–17 and 21, courtesy Magalen Ohrstrom Bryant; and pages 18, 70, and 95, courtesy Getty Images.
No part of this publication may be reproduced or transmitted in any form or by any means, electronic or mechanical, including photocopying, recording, or any information storage or retrieval system now known or to be invented, without written permission from Dover Corporation or its assigns.
First edition
Printed in Hong Kong

14 13 12 11 10 09 08 07 06 05   1 2 3 4 5

ISBN: 0-9749510-1-3

Fenwick Publishing Group, Inc.
292 Ericksen Avenue, Suite B
Bainbridge Island, Washington 98110

Fenwick Publishing produces, publishes, and markets custom publications for corporations, institutions, nonprofit organizations, and individuals.

www.fenwickpublishing.com

President and Publisher Timothy J. Connolly
Vice President, Development Sarah Morgans
Administrative Assistant Anna Joe Savage
Designers Kevin Berger and Kelly Pensell
Editor Pat Andrews
Proofreader Marco Pavia

TABLE OF CONTENTS

FOREWORD 12

CHAPTER ONE
FOUNDATIONS 14

CHAPTER TWO
TILT TOWARD GROWTH 60

CHAPTER THREE
LAUNCHING PAD 106

INDEX 152

ABOUT THE AUTHOR 159

Best-selling business author Ram Charan is renowned for the practical, real-world advice he offers to CEOs and boards of directors for some of the world's most successful companies. The coauthor of the landmark *Fortune* article "Why CEOs Fail," Charan is considered an expert on corporate governance, CEO succession, and strategy implementation.

FOREWORD

It is a privilege for me to write a foreword acknowledging the outstanding success of Dover Corporation over the past fifty years. This is a company that can be regarded as a jewel of America, one whose continued success sets it apart from so many manufacturing companies that are losing their edge. Largely focused on selected niches of manufacturing, Dover manufactures not just in the United States but all over the world—in places like China, India, parts of Latin America, and Eastern Europe—and it continues to expand and adapt in tune with growth in the global economy.

What makes Dover so exceptional? First, the high values inculcated in management and leadership from the top to the bottom. The ethics, behaviors, and work practices throughout Dover are of the highest standard. They create a positive, constructive work environment in which entrepreneurialism, commitment, and business savvy thrive.

Second, and unique to Dover, is its approach to improving performance, which allows the soundness of business decisions to overtake quarterly results. Dover creates value for shareholders not on the basis of meeting Wall Street's hunger for quarterly results but rather on the basis of improvement from year to year with an eye on three-year cycles, thus balancing the long-term and short-term. As performance rises on a business-cycle basis, people are rewarded accordingly. That is, incentives are based on a continuous three-year cycle and depend on genuine improvement in the business, not on performance against budgets. When Dover buys a selected niche manufacturing company, its intent is to keep it for the long run, and to build and improve it. Only occasionally is the portfolio mix changed when a particular company can be more beneficial to some other owner.

Dover's success also lies in the way top management leads operating company management. Headquarters gives subsidiary and operating company leaders great autonomy and freedom. Operating company managers have a total sense of ownership and, with it, a sense of responsibility. Their performance is based entirely on doing better than others in the marketplace, defined in terms of customer satisfaction, competitive advantage, and innovation, and they feel secure because they are self-driven to achieve. Success is measured not according to some accounting convention but primarily on a cash basis, which is the essential measure of success in any business, anywhere.

Dover Corporation's culture is the best assurance that the company will endure. Its gene pool is free of politics. It has high standards of ethics, honesty, and performance. Its leadership at all levels is motivated by improvement in business performance, and not by Wall Street. It builds collaboration from the ground up. And it continually adapts to structural changes in the environment. In my view, the secret of Dover's success over fifty years is the foundation for its success in the future.

Ram Charan

ALWAYS ENTREPRENEURSHIP The Dover Corporation was founded by George L. Ohrstrom, a man with integrity and an adventuresome spirit who had a clear vision that acquired companies should operate autonomously, and an operating company president should run the company as though he owned it. And, historically, it is from the operating companies that Dover CEOs have been chosen. Ohrstrom pulled the first CEO of the Dover Corporation from within, hiring Fred Durham, president of C. Lee Cook, one of the four pillar Dover companies. When it came time for his successor, Durham followed Ohrstrom's lead, elevating Tom Sutton, pictured above (center, with white tie), from his role as president of OPW—a position he had earned after starting as secretary to the sales manager—to CEO of Dover. The tradition of great leaders of vision chosen from within the Dover family continues today.

1 FOUNDATIONS

First, there was the founder. George L. Ohrstrom was a contradiction of sorts, a shy, private, humble Midwesterner who rode horses and hunted quail, yet exhibited the infinite charm and polished manners of the urbane. Handsome and patrician, with a prominent nose flanked by eyes that wore a bemused expression, Ohrstrom did not smoke and would not allow an ashtray in his office; nevertheless, he was inexorably drawn to the thrill of risk. A flying ace in World War I, he is credited with shooting down the last German plane prior to the armistice. When the war ended, he cast about for a profession as exhilarating as barnstorming, and found his life's calling in the intrepid business of finance.

FLYING ACE
During World War I, Dover founder George Ohrstrom, right, posed with the plane he flew when he shot down the last German plane before the armistice. His adventuresome, risk-taking days continued in the world of business finance.

DOVER CORPORATION FOUNDATIONS

CITY OF DREAMS

Business in New York City in 1926—the year this photo was taken—was bustling, especially for George Ohrstrom, who started up G. L. Ohrstrom & Company in the city to develop public utility companies. Three years later, Ohrstrom's company fell like many others.

In the early 1920s, Ohrstrom took a position selling securities at a Chicago brokerage firm that acquired and operated water companies. A dynamic salesman, by 1926 he had earned enough money to branch out on his own and established G. L. Ohrstrom & Company in New York City as an investment banking firm. It was the Roaring Twenties, a "can do" period of unbridled optimism, and Ohrstrom hoped to build a water holding company similar to the highly leveraged electric utilities then in vogue, which would retail water to residential households. By the end of the decade, he had developed not only several water holding companies but a few small public utilities as well, all of them highly leveraged. He had even formed a gas pipeline corporation and financed the construction of several office buildings in the downtown financial district. He had the Midas touch, and money from his various enterprises furnished him a lavish lifestyle that included a penthouse apartment atop 400 Madison Avenue.

But just as the name Ohrstrom started to gain currency on Wall Street, the stock market crashed in 1929, and George Ohrstrom learned the true meaning of risk. His highly leveraged investments were unable to meet their debt service and, as the Great Depression tightened its noose around the country, G. L. Ohrstrom & Company felt the pinch. "The operating companies could not earn enough to support the top-heavy debt structure, and the whole thing crashed," said Al Boustead, an accountant who had joined the firm only three months before the stock market's collapse. "We had to move from our elaborate quarters at 44 Wall Street with our private entrance . . . to a very small space. We had very little capital, and we were in the Depression."

Most men would retreat to less risky ventures, but not Ohrstrom. He promptly formed a second company and, in the early 1930s, turned his sights to buying industrials, which were even riskier than utilities. The company did "pretty well" for a few years, said Boustead, enabling it to move "upstairs to larger quarters." But an infraction cited by the United States Securities and Exchange Commission compelled Ohrstrom to liquidate the company in 1939. "George again lost everything—was out of business," Boustead said in a 1988 interview. "The Internal Revenue Service took everything we had."

Cautious but undeterred, Ohrstrom launched a third company, G. L. Ohrstrom & Associates, in 1946, this time as a limited partnership. Although the firm was organized as a broker-dealer, Ohrstrom could not resist the thrill of the buy, and he downplayed brokerage in favor of acquiring small industrial companies, employing the leveraging techniques he had refined with his water companies. His first acquisition was Peerless Manufacturing, a maker of industrial space heaters and fireplace equipment. In 1947, Ohrstrom acquired two more companies, Rotary Lift Company and Ohio Pattern Works (OPW). Rotary Lift had pioneered the development of hydraulic automobile lifts and had applied that knowledge to the manufacturing of hydraulic elevators. OPW had initially made grave markers and oil valves in the late nineteenth century but later found fortune as the manufacturer of automatic shut-off nozzles used to fuel automobiles. Ohrstrom further acquired W. C.

SECOND PILLAR
Rotary Lift, a manufacturer of automobile lifts, was acquired by George Ohrstrom in 1947 and became one of the four pillars creating Dover Corporation in 1955. Below: Rotary's circa-1960 two-plunger frame pickup lift.

DOVER CORPORATION FOUNDATIONS

LEADERSHIP: THE FOUNDER

George L. Ohrstrom was the son of Danish immigrants who had settled in Ford River, Michigan, where Ohrstrom, Dover's founder, was born in 1895. He attended the University of Michigan and then joined the American Expeditionary Services in World War I, distinguishing himself as the last American aviator to shoot down an enemy plane before the armistice in 1918. After the war, he took a job selling securities at P. W. Chapman & Company, a Chicago-based stock brokerage firm, when the thunder of the stampeding bull market lured him to New York City.

He established G. L. Ohrstrom & Company as an investment banking firm, and started acquiring water companies in highly leveraged deals, eventually forming Federal Water Service Company as a holding company for those concerns. He also developed a gas pipeline company and purchased several real estate properties, even sponsoring the construction of the Bank of Manhattan building at 40 Wall Street, which, at the time, was the world's tallest building.

By 1929, George Ohrstrom was at the top of the business world, considered one of the city's most important entrepreneurs, financiers, and leveraged-buyout experts. Ohrstrom's budding empire all came crashing down when the stock market

Norris, an oil well equipment manufacturer in Tulsa, Oklahoma, in 1950 and, in 1953, C. Lee Cook Manufacturing Company, producer of the first metallic packing used on piston rods for locomotives and steamships.

Those companies and Ohrstrom's other acquisitions during the 1950s produced highly dissimilar products and competed in vastly different markets. Yet, they all shared certain distinguishable features: In almost all cases, the companies made highly specialized, quality products for national markets; held the patents on their respective technologies; were market leaders; made products easily understood by their customers; did not sell products to retail markets; were dependably profit-able; and were small family or closely held concerns. Ohrstrom often said he would rather buy the dominant player in a small, niche industry than an also-ran in a large, highly competitive industry.

Money for the highly leveraged deals came from several sources, including two British merchant banks that had wagered on Ohrstrom investments in the 1920s, bank loans secured by inventory and accounts receivable, mortgage-backed financing from insurance companies, and cash from ongoing operations. Ohrstrom had neither the ability to manage the companies he acquired nor an interest in doing so; rather, he targeted businesses with strong operating leaders and insisted those leaders

imploded on Black Tuesday, October 29, 1929. As the Great Depression set in, G. L. Ohrstrom & Company endured great difficulty meeting its numerous outstanding obligations, and the weight of its debt eventually crushed it. "All went through the wringer," recalled Albert Boustead, the firm's accountant, in a 1981 interview.

Unlike many other financiers who left Wall Street for greener pastures after the crash, Ohrstrom stood firm and reinvented his business again and again. "He just couldn't sit still," Boustead said in 1988. "He was a very, very energetic man. . . . He had to be doing something all the time." Ohrstrom's sincerity in trying to meet his debt obligations to the two British merchant banks that held his securities solidified his reputation for integrity and responsibility and endeared him to the firms' principals. The banks continued to fund his business plans going forward, putting up as much as 75 percent of the capital, initially.

During his long career, George Ohrstrom made and lost two fortunes but his third firm, G. L. Ohrstrom & Associates, spawned two public companies, Dover Corporation and Carlisle Corporation, and continues to flourish decades after his death in 1955. GLO & Assocs. focuses exclusively on private equity investments, purchasing companies that manufacture a wide range of engineered products that serve the industrial, energy, aerospace, medical, and consumer markets. Today, the firm's chairman of the board is the founder's son, George L. Ohrstrom, Jr.

AN ACQUISITIVE MIND

George Ohrstrom was an accomplished businessman, the founder of what would become two large corporations—Dover and Carlisle Corporation. Ohrstrom became successful by buying small, well-managed companies and encouraging their autonomous management. Below: A portrait of Ohrstrom in riding regalia.

remain in place post-acquisition. He further assured them that he would not interfere with the continuing operations of their companies. And he stuck to his word. "The way that the Ohrstrom people treated me when I operated my old company for them was that they just left me alone," said Fred Durham, former owner of C. Lee Cook. "Ohrstrom had no particular interest in the company as such or how it operated or anything else. The operating of it was secondary."

Among Ohrstrom's numerous holdings in the 1950s was Carlisle Tire & Rubber, a publicly owned company that manufactured inner tubes and tires. Ohrstrom realized that, if he could sell some of his highly leveraged holdings to Carlisle, receiving shares of stock in return, he would control a much larger entity that would have greater access to capital from the equity markets, helping him fund the purchase of additional manufacturing companies. In January 1954, he merged Rotary Lift into the rechristened Carlisle Corporation, which would act as a diversified holding company for Ohrstrom's various interests.

Within months, however, frequent clashes between Carlisle's president and Hugh Allan, Rotary Lift's president, generated the need to create another company. In March 1955, Ohrstrom took Rotary Lift out of Carlisle

DOVER CORPORATION   FOUNDATIONS

THE SOUL OF DOVER
Fred Durham, in his office at C. Lee Cook, was first a metallurgist at Cook in 1923, then president and owner. After Dover's acquisition of Cook, he became Dover's first CEO, and also served as chairman for sixteen years. Inset: A 1955 ledger with entries for the four pillar companies.

and combined it with C. Lee Cook and W. C. Norris to form a second public company, Dover Corporation, named after the Delaware city—all without the use of an underwriter. In October 1955, Peerless Manufacturing was merged into the new company. Shares of Dover were distributed to Carlisle stockholders on the basis of one share of Dover for every four Carlisle shares owned— 136,500 shares in all. Dover ultimately became the larger and more prosperous of the two companies, and Rotary Lift, C. Lee Cook, W. C. Norris, and Peerless became the founding four operating companies—the four pillars, they are often called—of Dover Corporation.

Ohrstrom had no plans to preside over either Carlisle or Dover, reserving his efforts, instead, for the acquisition of more companies. To run Dover as its first chief executive, he selected Fred Durham, president and former owner of C. Lee Cook. But Durham was a reluctant candidate. His reason for selling C. Lee Cook to Dover two years earlier had been that his health was deteriorating and he wanted very much to retire to his home in Warsaw, Virginia, to cut timber and farm oysters. "That was about the extent of my ambition at the time. You plant oysters and don't see them anymore for three years to harvest time," he said in a 1989 interview. He had agreed to stay on at Cook for one year after the Dover acquisition, and only because his contract permitted Ohrstrom to retain him for an additional year did he stay longer.

"I don't know what you have in mind," he insisted to Ohrstrom, "but I can't see why you would choose me to run Dover because I sold my company in order to get out." His objections did little good. Durham caved in to Ohrstrom's charm and waited another sixteen years to farm his much-anticipated oysters, guiding Dover as its CEO and, later, its chairman through 1971.

Durham was warm and diplomatic, a "Southern gentleman" with a colloquial vernacular developed during his travels around the world on a tramp steamer in 1917 when he was just eighteen years old. He was tall and rangy, "a bean pole," he once said of himself. A metallurgical engineer by training, Durham's mentor had been Charles Lee Cook, founder of the C. Lee Cook company. Cook had hired Durham in 1923 to fabricate a more durable metal composite for the piston rings that his company made for gas-fueled engines.

Cook was one of the most extraordinary inventors of the late nineteenth and early twentieth centuries. A victim of polio, he had been wheelchair-bound since childhood and could move only his right hand; yet, he never let his disability deter his determination to succeed. In his lifetime, he was awarded several United States patents, became an accomplished linguist and painter, and even enjoyed the rare honor of addressing the United States Senate. "Self-pity is fatal to success," he told the legislators. "The way to meet difficulties is to face them." After Cook passed away in 1928, Durham bought C. Lee Cook from Cook's widow.

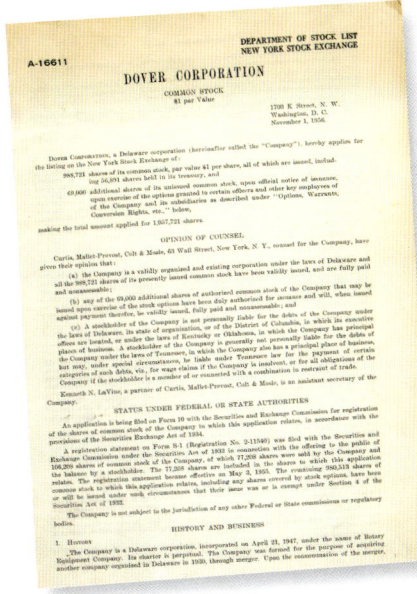

Cook was a pillar of uprightness, and his principles rubbed off on Durham, whom Cook considered his protégé. "He insisted upon complete integrity, that you don't lie and you don't cheat," Durham said. To Durham, integrity also meant intellectual honesty, plain-spoken candor, an ability to evaluate one's own weaknesses and strengths, and a desire to remain free of ego and detached from political infighting. Those qualities of Durham's character and personal philosophy would come to describe Dover's future leadership.

Ohrstrom promised Durham that the CEO position would be "temporary" and that Durham would soon be able to return to his Virginia home. He even allowed Durham to run Dover from Durham's C. Lee Cook offices in Louisville, Kentucky. Ohrstrom's promise was short-lived: On November 10, 1955, Ohrstrom was stricken with a fatal heart attack. He had spent the morning riding to the hounds and died "with his boots on," his daughter, Maggie Ohrstrom Bryant, said. He was sixty-one years old. It was up to Durham now, as Dover's chairman and CEO, to forge a successful, profitable corporation from the various enterprises that Ohrstrom had combined for purely financial reasons. "My main duties as I saw them were to establish a headquarters, staff it and lay out a program of management, get Dover listed on the New York Stock Exchange, and so on," he wrote.

TAKING STOCK

Dover Corporation, founded in 1955, went public in 1956. Under the DOV symbol, Dover Corporation was listed on the venerable New York Stock Exchange. A single share of Dover stock, purchased on or before November 15, 1961, equaled almost 208 shares in May 2004. Assuming a shareholder had reinvested all the dividends through the years, by 2004 a single share of Dover stock, purchased at its original value of $18.12, was worth almost $13,000.

DOVER CORPORATION FOUNDATIONS

LEADERSHIP: THE FIRST CEO

Fred Durham, the first chief executive of Dover Corporation, was born in 1899 in rural Virginia. He was a typical farm boy of the era: His father owned and operated saw mills, a grist mill, a country store, and several farms, and young Durham performed numerous farm chores, from tilling the earth to harvesting the crop. Although his father died when Durham was twelve years old, Durham learned "the necessity of hard work and complete integrity," Durham stated in a 1988 interview.

After eight years at "country school," as he called it, Durham boarded away at King and Queen High School in Stevensville, Virginia, where he nurtured his budding interest in mechanics. His father had owned one of the first motorcars in the state, a Model T, which Durham drove and studied from the age of ten. He also mastered the mechanics of an old gasoline engine that powered a river-going vessel used to ferry lumber to sailing ships making their way to the bustling city of Baltimore.

After graduating from King and Queen, Durham went to Virginia Polytechnic Institute in Blacksburg, where he majored in mechanical engineering and studied metallurgy. Health problems—he was plagued by boils—tormented him during his junior year, and he decided to stay out of school temporarily in favor of an around-

Durham swiftly met those immediate needs, moving Dover's headquarters to 1700 K Street in Washington, D.C., largely because that location was within commuting distance of his home in Virginia. He assembled a small staff of two: Helen Root as secretary and Robert "Bob" Bethe as financial officer. Their barebones corporate headquarters consisted of two offices, a reception area, a small boardroom, a couple of telephones, bare floors, and little furniture. On December 3, 1956, Dover was listed on the New York Stock Exchange. Durham was present on the floor of the exchange to buy the first one hundred shares at roughly $5.60 per share.

As for a management strategy, Durham had no intention of tinkering with the divisional independence and decentralized management implicit in Ohrstrom's somewhat loose style. Rather, he would institute those concepts as managerial principles, which would come to be known as the Dover Philosophy. He did not want a return to the days when headquarters handed down edicts that minions mindlessly obeyed. Rather, Durham believed independent operations, run autonomously by former owners and managers, would allow those managers more control over solving their own problems, which they were more familiar with than anyone else. That independence, Durham believed, would encourage

the-world adventure aboard a tramp steamer. "I was in what they call the 'black gang'—working in the engine room," he said. "Then, over in Algiers, the third assistant engineer had to go to the hospital for an appendix operation, and we left him over there. And because I had some engineering training, they gave me an 'emergency license' to act as third assistant engineer on the way back from Africa to America."

Upon his return, he finished VPI and in 1922 took a job with Southern Bell Telephone Company in Atlanta, installing phones and "climbing a lot of poles," he grimly recalled. Shortly thereafter, the company relocated Durham to Louisville, Kentucky, as a toll engineer. One day in 1923, his boss, Tom Carr, invited him to a luncheon honoring Charles Lee Cook, one of the foremost inventors of the nineteenth and early twentieth centuries.

At the luncheon, Cook questioned Durham about Durham's life and work. When Durham mentioned his studies in metallurgy, Cook commented that his company was having difficulty with the durability of its metal products. A few days later, Cook offered Durham a job as his chief engineer. Durham's task: Improve the permanence of piston rods. Through trial and error, Durham created Cook Graphitic Iron, a metal with much longer-lasting qualities. When Cook died in 1928, Durham bought the company from Cook's widow.

Durham ran C. Lee Cook for the next twenty-seven years, through 1955, and oversaw Dover Corporation as chief executive officer and chairman of the board through 1971, when he retired from the chairmanship. He died at his farm in Warsaw, Virginia, in 1998, at the age of ninety-eight.

NEVER MINCED A WORD

Fred Durham was on a bus with George Ohrstrom, when Ohrstrom asked him to be the first CEO of Dover. Durham was planning on retiring, but his plans soon changed—at the urging of Ohrstrom—and he accepted the position. Left: A portrait of Durham and Durham's gold engraved pen.

responsibility and inspire initiative, ingenuity, and entrepreneurialism. Not that hands-off oversight was in his blood. "At Cook, I was the most autocratic person," he once commented. "But I found out pretty quickly that I could not go around telling the [heads of Dover's constituent companies] how to do everything."

Durham also had neither the staff nor the expertise at corporate headquarters to make decisions for the four divisions—Rotary Lift, W. C. Norris, C. Lee Cook, and Peerless Manufacturing. Consequently, he advised that the divisions "boss themselves," he explained in a speech before the New York Society of Security Analysts in 1956. "We believe in selecting a capable manager and then giving him complete responsibility for his division, from personnel to production and sales," Durham stated. On another occasion, he wrote, "Our only assurance that the operations will be run well now and tomorrow is to have good men in key positions at each division."

Autonomy did not mean liberty to operate on a subpar basis, however. While the divisions were free to operate their businesses as they saw fit, their decisions were subject to evaluation, especially in the area of financial discipline. To appraise divisional performance, Durham and Bethe established central oversight controls and responsibilities: Divisions were required to post to Dover's

DOVER CORPORATION FOUNDATIONS

CULTURE: THE DOVER PHILOSOPHY

It has been called a simple, elegant formula for success—a set of singular operating principles that distinguish Dover from other large conglomerates. The Dover Philosophy, as this formula is known, has a proven track record of fifty years. It was developed somewhat serendipitously, spawned from the detailed acquisition criteria established by Dover's founder, George L. Ohrstrom.

A pioneer in the conglomerate movement of the 1950s, Ohrstrom had a distinctive approach to acquisitions—buying small family-owned or closely held companies that manufactured products for niche markets that he readily understood. Typically, those companies were national market leaders with an impressive track record of earnings, and sold products to industrial buyers rather than to the public at large. Finally, management of the companies was in the hands of skilled individuals who were eager to continue in their roles after the acquisition.

Take the case of OPW, which G. L. Ohrstrom & Associates acquired in 1948 and sold to Dover in 1961: OPW had invented the automatic shut-off nozzle for dispensing fuel at service stations, for which it was awarded a United States patent. The company was well known in the petroleum equipment market and had leading market share nationally. Over the decades since the company's founding in 1892, OPW's managers had forged a vertically integrated company that made all its products from scratch. It boasted a machine shop, full assembly operation, and dedicated foundry that made castings for the company's own use. OPW was the dominant player in a small, niche industry. In short, it was the perfect Dover candidate.

When buying companies, Ohrstrom had no strategic theory of diversification; he did not, for example, look for companies whose markets were countercyclical. He simply sought out successful manufacturers that fit the Dover mold. He also had no recorded intent to derive synergies from his holdings, such as he would have by creating central offices for purchasing, sales, and marketing. He was a financier first and foremost, and had no interest in running far-flung companies via layers of centralized management bureaucracy. His job, as he saw it, was to continue to buy companies that met his criteria and leave the management of his companies to the people in charge of running them.

Ohrstrom, who died in the same year as Dover's founding, never had the opportunity to refine the Dover Philosophy. That was left to Dover's first chief executive, Fred Durham. Durham had presided over the C. Lee Cook Manufacturing Company for twenty-seven years before Ohrstrom bought that company in 1953, but he had no desire to interfere with the management of Dover's constituent companies. He believed strongly that operating independence and autonomous management would inspire entrepreneurialism, initiative, and responsibility. As for Dover's corporate role—the oversight responsibility of all publicly traded companies—Durham retained a lean, informal central office staff and unimposing quarters. The staff's job was to monitor Dover's constituent companies through uniform accounting systems and financial reports without prescribing a means to desired financial ends.

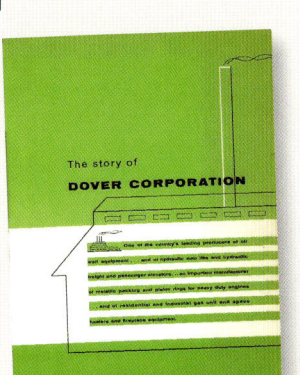

Through the years, Durham's successors have adhered closely to the principles of the Dover Philosophy. Although the acquisition criteria have broadened to accommodate the growth needs of a multibillion dollar global corporation, and Dover's central office staff is marginally larger, the primary tenets of the Dover Philosophy—decentralized operations and autonomous management—continue to define the corporation today. Upon Durham's retirement, his colleagues honored him with these words: "Dover Corporation owes its success, character, and, in large measure, its future to the management philosophy and practices of one man: Fred Durham. He believes that business, like any other human enterprise, thrives best where creativity and initiative are encouraged in an atmosphere of maximum autonomy."

corporate office monthly profit and loss statements, daily reports of cash flow and inventory backlog, and requests for capital expenditures above $5,000. Those requirements, Bethe believed, would motivate the divisions "to do a much better job of analysis than was the case prior to the formation of Dover," he said in a 1988 interview.

At Dover headquarters, Durham was equally accommodating, letting his staff make their own decisions about how they would do their work, and emphasizing a no-frills, no-nonsense, nonbureaucratic corporate participation in planning, and no routine investigations of operating practices—the norm at other multi-industry companies. "The chief reason for our method of management was to retain the flexibility and initiative that had made the division heads leaders in their industries in the first place," explained Bethe, who was named controller in 1956.

To preserve the entrepreneurial spirit of independent

"RUN YOUR COMPANIES AS IF YOU OWN THEM. IF IT WORKS, YOU ARE GOING TO GET CREDIT FOR IT. IF IT FAILS, IT MAY BE YOUR ASS."

—Fred Durham, Dover Corporation Chairman and CEO (1955–1971)

atmosphere. Headquarters was in charge of overall policy, finance, acquisitions, executive personnel, and administrative details, such as insurance and pension plans, which Durham believed were better handled centrally. Other areas of corporate concentration were taxes, borrowings, shareholder relations, and board relations. Dover's head office also retained responsibility for approving the selection of top division executives and consulted with divisions on product development, research programs, and labor issues to ensure those plans fit into long-term corporate objectives.

Still, that oversight was far from invasive—there were no regular audits of the divisions, no extensive management, Durham also resisted any efforts to effect vertical integration or corporate synergies, such as through centralized purchasing or intracorporate management. Intercompany loans were forbidden and, in situations where constituent companies purchased products from one another, they were required to pay competitive prices. In addition, Dover's future acquisitions were opportunistic, with little regard for balancing market cyclicality or achieving synergies as was the policy of most conglomerates. "We'd have people say, 'Why not buy this foundry and have it make castings for all your companies?'" recalls Tony Ormsby, who joined Dover's corporate office as vice president in early 1963. "'Look at

RIGHT-HAND MAN
Bob Bethe (right), Dover's first controller, and Fred Durham worked closely together in Dover's office. Durham relied on Bethe, who was in charge of monitoring the financial performance of Dover's constituent companies, to figure out the financial details of the business.

PUMPING IRON

In 1964, Dover acquired Blackmer Pump, a maker of positive displacement pumps for the petroleum and general industries. Here, a worker operates an electric furnace that pours molten metal into a cast to fashion the company's signature product.

DOVER CORPORATION   FOUNDATIONS

BIRD'S-EYE VIEW
Although Dover has always kept a watchful eye on operating company performance, headquarters does not interfere with operations. Management is left to the company president—a practice that proved prosperous for Rotary Lift. Above: Rotary Lift's sprawling Memphis, Tennessee, plant, circa 1960.

the money you're wasting.' But it was not Dover's job to consider this, only the divisions.'"

The only synergy that mattered to Durham was the economic balance that could be achieved through "the inherent advantages of diversification," he told the security analysts in his 1956 speech. By eschewing a shared Dover identity and by insisting upon divisional independence, Durham believed he could create pride, loyalty, and a long-term view at the divisional level.

To check up on the divisions, Durham or Bethe would make periodic visits, asking questions of division leaders rather than giving answers. "It certainly is not for me to say, 'Look, this is not the way to do it. Do it this way,'" Durham said. "Then, what's he sitting there for? I might as well fire him and tell these guys myself. I'm playing checkers over his shoulder and still expect him to take credit or blame for the results." Durham invited division presidents to "run your companies as if you own them. If it works, you are going to get credit for it. If it fails, it may be your ass."

It was left up to Bethe, a detail-oriented financial officer, to consolidate divisional data for the benefit of Dover's executive committee, which had general oversight responsibility for the allocation of financial resources and the annual budget preparation process. The committee—George Ohrstrom's son, Ricard; Merrill Stubbs, a partner in G. L. Ohrstrom & Company; and Durham—joined the four division presidents in the makeup of Dover's board of directors, which abdicated the customary oversight obligations to the executive committee.

As in all conglomerates, growth at Dover was achieved both internally within the divisions and through acquisitions. Responsibility for finding and making acquisitions was split three ways, with the executive committee, corporate office, and divisions all participating. Each scouted companies fitting Dover's precise acquisition criteria—owner-managed, profitable, high-performance companies in simple-to-understand businesses that sold highly engineered and predominantly proprietary products in limited, well-defined, industrial markets in which they had a leading market share. "We are continually investigating the possibility of acquiring additional companies to diversify further our operations, increase our earnings potential, and strengthen our position in certain markets," Durham stated in Dover's 1959 annual report.

By becoming part of Dover, companies were assured they would gain better access to capital than if they were to remain private and independent. Capital could be directed to new product development, plant expansion, and more modern equipment, Dover told acquisition candidates. And Dover stood behind its word: In 1957, for example, it financed the building of the world's most modern sucker rod plant for W. C. Norris at a cost of more than $2 million.

Although acquisition candidates were required to sustain historical results and pay off any outstanding loans against their assets, their managements would continue to operate as they had before acquisition, largely free of corporate interference. It was a tantalizing inducement; and, over the course of Durham's tenure as CEO, Dover made seventeen acquisitions. The executive committee selected three companies in which G. L. Ohrstrom had interests—Dura-Vent, a producer of gas vent pipe for gas heaters; OPW; and Walter O'Bannon, a subsurface oil well pump producer. The corporate office selected two: Blackmer Pump, a leading manufacturer of positive displacement pumps, centrifugal pumps, and compressors; and DE-STA-CO Industries, a principal maker of reed valves and toggle clamps. Divisions selected the remaining twelve, which were largely product- and/or service-line acquisitions.

Most of the divisional acquisitions were in the elevator sector. Rotary Lift had broadened its market from hydraulic automobile lifts to hydraulic elevators, and was seeking to become a major player in the elevator field. In 1958, Dover acquired Shepard-Warner Elevator, which made geared-traction elevators and "stair climbers," the early version of escalators, thereby complementing Rotary's line. The company also provided elevator installation, service, and maintenance; thus, the combined Dover-held elevator operation could effectively serve a wide variety of market needs.

In 1960, Dover separated elevator operations out of the Rotary Lift division and formed a new, fifth division, Dover Elevator Company, leaving Rotary solely in the car lift business. Gradually, the "Dover" symbol replaced the bright red and mustard-yellow Rotary Lift symbol on elevator company advertising brochures. Hugh Allan, formerly the head of Rotary, was named the president of the new division. Given authority to make add-on acquisitions, Allan eventually expanded the division's product line and territory. Over the years, he and his successors developed Dover Elevator into the elevator industry's third largest company.

Five years into his tenure as head of Dover, Durham made a decision he would forever regard as one of his biggest mistakes. He had often asserted to the division presidents that picking a capable successor was a critical long-term decision for anyone

ADDING IT UP
By 1959, Dover's annual report sported the company's new logo and listed five divisions and three subsidiaries, up from the four original divisions listed in Dover's first annual report in 1955.

PORTFOLIO POWER

A listing of various Ohrstrom interests in 1957, below, contains some still-familiar operating company names and highlights the expansive growth of the Dover Corporation, which today boasts more than fifty operating companies.

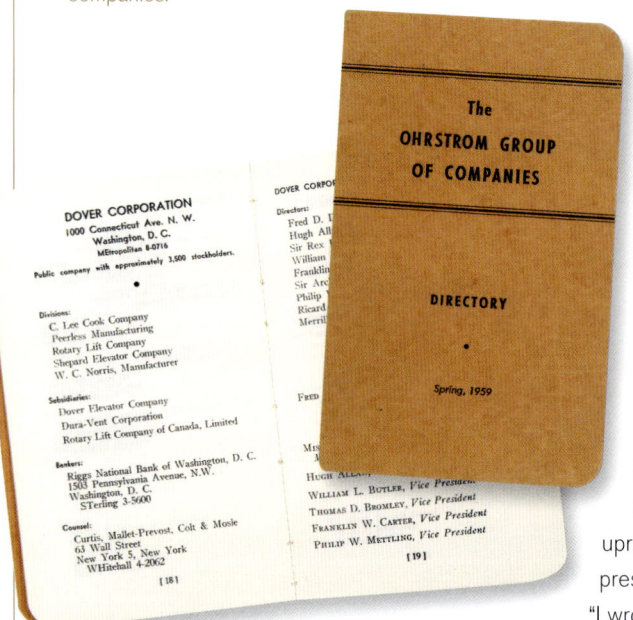

managing a growing business; hence, he encouraged the presidents to identify their own replacements from within their organizations well in advance of their retirements and to groom the identified successors for the job. However, in selecting his own successor in 1961, Durham cast his net outside Dover to hire Otto Schwenk, an executive from a more traditional, large, hierarchical company.

The decision proved disastrous: Schwenk sought to transform Dover into a conventional centralized, bureaucratic company with a large staff and functional vice presidents for manufacturing, marketing, purchasing, industrial relations, and sales, whose jobs were to advise the divisions. He also planned to move Dover headquarters to much grander quarters in Pittsburgh and to outfit the offices with lavish furniture and appointments. Most ominously, Schwenk broke the cardinal rule of autonomous management—interfering with decisions made by division heads. "Schwenk's interference incited a palace uprising," recalled Thomas Sutton, president of OPW at the time. "I wrote a letter to Fred [Durham, still Dover's chairman] saying, 'I quit.' There was no way I was going to continue to work for Schwenk. He didn't understand the value of operating freedom to people who were on the firing line dealing daily with customers and problems, thinking he could do this better than anyone else could."

One year into the job, Schwenk was asked to hand in his resignation. Said Durham, "He couldn't let the managers manage."

The Dover credo of divisional independence and autonomous management endured another test when managerial problems at W. C. Norris surfaced in 1960. The market for oil drilling equipment had become depressed, but the division's president had no viable strategy for attacking the situation. Rather than immediately replacing the president, a tactic the board of directors recommended, Durham held fast. By 1963 conditions at the company had worsened; he had no other option than to fire the man. Durham learned a valuable lesson: A willingness to stomach mistakes to preserve divisional leadership has a serious price. In the future, Dover would formulate remedies for dealing with subpar results at an ailing division, beginning with the replacement of the president and ending with the last resort—divestiture.

The early 1960s were an age of confidence in the United States. Americans had more jobs and more income at their disposal, and were flocking to the suburbs to live in new homes with two-car garages and manicured lawns. New businesses sprouted and, with them, new buildings. Dover was well poised to take advantage of a veritable boom in building starts, which opened up important opportunities for its elevator business.

In 1963, Dover recorded record net earnings of $4.25 million, representing an 18.6 percent return on shareholder equity—a return higher than that of 95 percent of the Fortune 500 industrial companies. The next year was even better: Dover's net earnings reached

AUTONOMY: UP, UP, AND AWAY

The history of Dover Elevator Company begins during the Great Depression. In the early 1930s, Rotary Lift Company, one of the four original companies to form Dover Corporation in 1955, was struggling with a decline in sales of its signature product—hydraulic automobile lifts. Hugh Allan, who had just joined Rotary's sales department, offered an idea about how to weather the difficult period: Diversify into the making of hydraulic freight elevators.

Hydraulic elevators had been invented in France in the 1850s, but their day seemed long over when Allan pitched his idea. Geared-traction elevators were the "new technology," and they had quickly dominated the field. Allan was convinced, however, that Rotary could resuscitate the fortunes of the hydraulic elevator by applying Rotary's singular engineering expertise in hydraulic machinery to the declining line. After some discussion, Rotary's management backed the concept, as long as Allan began modestly with only a few customers to test the waters. The task then fell to Rotary's engineers to develop the new product.

Their first model was a direct-acting hydraulic elevator that was sold to a supermarket in Rotary's hometown of Memphis, Tennessee, but the elevator was tiny and prone to breaking down. The engineers then unveiled the world's first oil hydraulic elevator for Rotary's second customer, Texas A&M College, which had ordered two: One was for the school's new science building; the other was a circular elevating and rotating platform for an amphitheater classroom. The new line, later called the Oildraulic, used oil instead of water as the hydraulic fluid, thereby greatly reducing friction and the chief complaint of hydraulic elevators—noise. The relative quiet of Rotary's elevator had great appeal to its next customer, an independent New York company that provided elevators to mortuaries.

Business built incrementally, and in 1936 Rotary's officers agreed the company should officially enter the hydraulic elevator field with a full line backed by separate sales and marketing. The company soon landed its first big contract, New York's Airlines Terminal Building, which needed a giant elevator to lift buses from street level to the lobby of the terminal for loading and unloading. The building's architects deemed a traction elevator too costly for the project, and Rotary nailed the contract. Many additional large contracts followed, including one for servicing apartment buildings, opera houses, and even missile-launching platforms.

Rotary Lift was bought by G. L. Ohrstrom & Associates in 1947. George Ohrstrom later combined Rotary and three of his other holdings into Dover Corporation in 1955, naming Hugh Allan as Rotary's president. Over the next several years, Dover's capital funded the acquisition of numerous other elevator companies, broadening Rotary's product line to include traction elevators and adding elevator installation, service, and maintenance capabilities.

In 1960, the elevator line was cleaved from Rotary Lift and renamed Dover Elevator Company. The irony is that, unlike the other companies that Dover had acquired and the hundreds it would accumulate over its first fifty years, Dover Elevator, which grew to become Dover's largest company at one time, was internally developed. Under Hugh Allan, whose idea it had been in the first place, Dover Elevator grew to become the industry's third largest company, just behind Otis and Westinghouse. Although Dover Corporation sold Dover Elevator Company to Germany's Thyssen Industrie in 1998 for $1.1 billion, to this day hundreds, if not thousands, of elevators around the United States still carry the name Dover.

DOVER CORPORATION FOUNDATIONS

a new high of $6 million, and its sales increased to $84 million from $27 million in the company's first full year of business. Under Durham's guidance from 1955 to 1964, Dover's annual compound growth rate in revenues was 17.7 percent and in profits, 13.7 percent. The 1964 annual report describes the diversified company's business as embracing six major markets, though its fortunes rested heavily on prospects in the oil fields and the construction markets at that time.

Durham's ultimate successor as Dover's CEO was Tom Sutton, OPW president. In the years ahead, Sutton would steer Dover toward further diversification in its portfolio of operating companies without disrupting the cardinal tenets of the Dover Philosophy as Schwenk had attempted to do. Sutton and Durham were of one mind on the corporate management strategy.

Durham appointed Sutton executive vice president in 1963. "We clicked insofar as our minds and thinking were concerned," Durham said. To prepare Sutton for the CEO spot, Durham dispatched him to England to confer with Dover's British investors and, later, to the Dover divisions to get a feel for their operations and to meet with their presidents. "They are the ones you will work with and through," Durham wrote to Sutton. "Each has his strong and his weak points. Some even have blind spots; thus, you must know how they manage, which areas they give most attention to and which they neglect. The better you know them, the more effective you will be."

MENTOR AND PROTÉGÉ
Fred Durham, standing, and Tom Sutton—Dover's first and second CEO, respectively—enjoyed a long business relationship and close friendship that lasted until the time of Durham's death in 1998 at the age of ninety-eight.

MANAGEMENT MATERIAL

Starting out as secretary to the vice president of sales at OPW, Tom Sutton honed a straightforward management style and unwavering integrity, which aided him as CEO of Dover. Left: Sutton stands with then-Norris sucker rod plant manager Harold Bell on Norris's manufacturing floor.

Sutton officially became Dover president and CEO in May 1964; Durham remained as chairman of the board. A handwritten letter from Sutton to Durham upon his appointment as CEO stated, "Thanks for the opportunity to 'try out' for the job at corporate headquarters. Thanks, most of all, for the opportunity to work with you." The two men would work closely together in the years ahead, developing a mutual respect and friendship that would last a lifetime. In a 2004 interview, Sutton commented, "You might say I adopted Fred as my father." Durham concurred: "If I could have been blessed with a son and had a chance to pick him, Tom Sutton would have been it."

The "son" was the ideal candidate for the job. Born in 1921, Sutton served as a fighter pilot in North Africa, Italy, and England during World War II. After the war, he earned a bachelor's degree in accounting, using the G.I. Bill, and, while still a student at the University of Cincinnati, formed a company that made pottery mugs and ashtrays for fraternities and sororities. Although the venture failed, it gave Sutton a taste for running his own company. After another start-up had gone under, he got a job at OPW and worked his way up from the bottom of the ladder as the secretary to vice president of sales and finally to the top rung as president. "I knew the names of everyone there, whether they were in the machine shop, assembly department, or the corporate offices, and I would remember their wives' names, too," Sutton says.

With his pug nose, small stature, and bantam-rooster vigor, Sutton resembled the tough-guy actor

DOVER CORPORATION FOUNDATIONS

> **INNOVATION:** OPW'S AUTOMATIC SHUT-OFF NOZZLE
>
> For more than a century, OPW has been the market leader in the design, development, production, and support of fueling components and systems. Its long history boasts an extraordinary number of industry firsts, such as the first automatic shut-off valve, earning OPW Fueling Components more patents than any other petroleum equipment company. In 1949, OPW received a U.S. patent for the automatic shut-off nozzle. Prior to the development of the nozzle, it was touch and go for service station personnel to determine whether or not a consumer's gas tank was full. Spillage was a constant threat, creating maintenance and safety issues. OPW's 1811 nozzle shut off automatically when the nozzle received a signal that the tank was full. The shut-off was accomplished by the creation of a vacuum generated by the flow of fuel through the nozzle. In 1970, OPW improved upon the 1811, which required two hands to operate, with the first one-hand-operated service station nozzle.

SERVING THE CUSTOMER

Tom Sutton's successors at OPW continued the company's tradition of customer-centric inventions, including the more user-friendly automatic shut-off valve dispensing nozzle. Right: A sampling of OPW brochures from the 1970s.

James Cagney. But it was his integrity more than his other characteristics that captivated Durham. "He is the only human being whom I've been closely associated with who treats everybody the same," Durham said. "Tom would treat a beggar on the street as if he were dealing with Churchill."

Sutton possessed an important attribute of leadership: the ability to be clear, simple, and straightforward at all times with all people. "Tom was a brilliant manager with a superb ability to communicate with people and open them up," Tony Ormsby says. "He created a climate of trust at the divisions." He also was sincerely interested in the "nuts and bolts" of each Dover division—their methods of manufacturing and other processes, even more so than their financial targets. "Tom understood everything about a business almost instantaneously because he lived through it all at OPW," Ormsby adds. "He forced himself through every job there. And, like Durham, he was neither inflexible nor ego-driven. He never sought power for the sake of power."

When Durham handed Sutton the reins to Dover, he uttered four words: "Don't f—— it up." (As he stated in a 1988 interview, "I can't talk without profanity. Never was able to.") The phrase has become company lore. "That said it all for me," Sutton said. "Fred was giving me this successful company, and he wanted me to know that I was its steward." He would continue to rely on Durham's advice throughout his career, even after Durham stepped down as chairman in 1971. "We'd talk at least once a month," Sutton recalled.

CENTER OF IT ALL
Tom Sutton relocated Dover's headquarters to the center of New York City's buzzing business district in 1964 to be closer to Dover's legal representation and, especially, the investment banking community. New York City remains Dover's corporate home today.

DOVER CORPORATION FOUNDATIONS

38

APPETIZING ACQUISITION

In 1967, Dover acquired Groen, a Chicago-based manufacturer of metal products, such as kettles and food processors, used predominantly in commercial kitchens and by the pharmaceutical industry.

In December 1964, Sutton relocated Dover headquarters to 277 Park Avenue in New York City to be closer to its legal representation and accountants, and, most importantly, to the investment banking community. Under Sutton, Dover would rely less on its executive committee to ferret out and make acquisitions and more on its New York executive staff. The shift was a bold departure from the past, and it helped launch Dover as an independent enterprise rather than just another Ohrstrom interest.

To assist him in developing and executing a "growth through acquisition" strategy, Sutton initially relied upon G. L. Ohrstrom and Associates as his liaison with Wall Street. Then, in 1967, he made one of his most important hiring decisions, recruiting former McKinsey & Company consultant W. Cameron Caswell. Caswell had attended Yale University and had wanted to be a surgeon but went to New York instead "to seek my fortune," he said in a 1988 interview. As Dover's director of long-range planning, Caswell applied his diagnostic skills to identifying acquisition prospects. "He was the 'intellect' of Dover," said Sutton, "in charge of finding companies."

Although the responsibility for acquisitions had shifted, the acquisition criteria remained the same: "No mining companies, no distribution companies, and so forth, just manufacturing companies, essentially metal-working, with relatively low technology," Caswell states. "It also had to be profitable and have management in place that would be there for at least three years. We also never bought companies that needed strong headquarters support because we didn't have it. And we didn't have it because we didn't need it. All we had to do was to keep doing what we'd been doing—in more places."

Sutton pursued a more ambitious and active acquisitions policy than Durham. From 1965 to 1970, Dover acquired five companies: Groen Manufacturing Company, a maker of restaurant kettles and related equipment; Ronningen-Petter, a manufacturer of filtration equipment and supplies used predominantly by the paper industry; Bernard Company, a manufacturer of gas welding guns and other products for the metal-fabrication market; and two elevator companies. One business newspaper called Dover an "acquisition express" in those years.

But Caswell said that he and Sutton "actually walked away from a lot of deals," noting that in 1967 Dover evaluated hundreds of companies as potential acquisitions and talked seriously to twenty-five before opting to buy only one—Groen. "Cam [Caswell] would find the deal and sell them on Dover; then I'd go in and take a look at the business," Sutton said, "And, if everything looked fine, . . . I would do the negotiation and Bob [Bethe] would do the financial support work and some business analysis."

The pitch to acquisition targets had not changed: Management would gain access to Dover capital to grow their businesses while retaining control of operations—or, as Sutton put it, they would have "no corporate staff to police their organizations." It was a tantalizing proposal, of course. Former assistant controller Fred Suesser recalls: "I remember the owner of Bernard, when his son asked him why he was selling the company, replied, 'Son, here is your fire truck. If I gave you ten dollars for it and said you can still play with it as much as you want, would you take the ten dollars?' Few wouldn't."

DOVER ALCHEMY

During Sutton's reign, Dover was primarily focused on acquiring metal-working manufacturing companies—a practice that initially lent to the success of Dover. Below: A metal Dover belt buckle.

DOVER CORPORATION FOUNDATIONS

LEADERSHIP: THE PILOT

"I was born in 1921 in Longmont, Colorado, but my family moved to Orange County, California, before my first birthday." So began Tom Sutton in a 2004 interview at his Dover office in Manhattan several months before his death on December 28, 2004. Sutton, Dover's long-running chief executive from 1964 to 1981, recalled his early life growing up in a region mythologized as a land of orange groves and movie stars.

Sutton's father was an engineer for a refrigeration company. Although Sutton and his dad were close, he considers his mother his true guiding influence. "Movies were a big industry in Southern California, and she insisted I take dancing lessons," Sutton said. "I guess she probably saw me as a great movie star someday. But the real bonus of performing was that it gave me terrific confidence in front of people."

Lithe, strong, and nimble, he studied ballroom dancing, was profiled in a local newspaper as "Orange County's Youngest Exhibitionist," and appeared in a tap and tumbling routine with a friend at the Palomar and the Palladium.

But stardom did not beckon Sutton. He attended junior college for a year and a half and then, as war broke out across the Atlantic, enlisted in the United States Army Air Corps. Although he had never flown in a plane, he signed up to be a fighter

Acquisition candidates skeptical about Dover's proposal were urged to contact Dover division heads to satisfy themselves. When they did, they typically were completely assured of Dover's pledge. "The path of several . . . acquisition negotiations was smoothed by the candid remarks of divisional presidents who had previously sold their own companies to Dover," remarked Sutton.

Not all acquisitions were success stories. Dover's first acquisition, Dura-Vent, which had been an Ohrstrom start-up and was the only Dover company that sold product retail, was divested in a management buy-out in 1966. Nevertheless, Dover was a reluctant seller of companies in the Sutton era, continuing Durham's strategy of first replacing the president of a below-par division and then, if that failed to improve company results, considering a divestiture as the very last resort. Indeed, Dover would not divest another division until Peerless in 1977.

Sutton reinforced the "small company" principles of the Dover Philosophy, leaving the strategies for attacking markets or gaining competitive advantage to the division heads, trusting they would make the right decisions. "There was no way in hell I could know as much about sucker rods as the guy running Norris or about auto lifts as the guy running Rotary," Sutton

pilot, was dispatched to flying school, and graduated as an officer in the Air Corps. When Japanese aircraft bombed Pearl Harbor and the United States subsequently entered the war, Sutton was assigned to a squadron that flew out of Cairo to perform bombing missions in Northern Africa and Europe. "There was a lot of dive bombing and close support work, and I was shot at but never downed," he recalled. "Altogether, I flew 108 missions."

After the war, Sutton finished college, earning a degree in accounting. While at school, he, his brother-in-law, and a friend—all war veterans—started a pottery manufacturing company that sold mugs and ashtrays to fraternities. It was called TAVCO, for Three Ambitious Veterans. The venture failed, but it gave Sutton a taste for running his own business. He launched another small company called Tinker Products, which made such decorative items as planters and sconces for florists and gifts shops, But money was scarce, and when Cincinnati-based OPW offered him a job in 1951, Sutton put aside his plans to run his own company and signed on as secretary to the vice president of sales. When Dover Corporation bought OPW from G. L. Ohrstrom & Associates in 1961, Sutton was vice president of sales. OPW's president, Gil Richards, had died the previous year but succession had not yet been established. Fred Durham, Dover's chief executive, met Sutton and made him president of OPW in 1962.

The job did not last long: The following year, Durham tapped Sutton to be his own executive vice president. In May 1964, Sutton was officially named Dover's president and chief executive officer. Said Durham, "The best thing I ever did for this company was to appoint Tom Sutton."

GROWTH THROUGH ACQUISITION

In 1964, Dover CEO and president Tom Sutton, right, had one thing on his mind—growing the corporation. Sutton pursued a more ambitious acquisition program than Fred Durham, acquiring five companies in his first five years at the wheel. Below: A key chain produced for OPW.

explained. "I learned that from Fred. You need to keep decision-making close to the customer."

He also rejected arguments concerning the cost efficiency of centralized operations and activities, such as hiring salesmen to market products for several Dover divisions. Like Durham, Sutton did not budge from his conviction in the value of complete divisional autonomy, believing that centralized intrusions into divisional operations snuff out initiative and injure morale. "Human initiative and ingenuity produce the best results when they are given the greatest possible freedom," he stated in Dover's 1965 annual report. In a subsequent interview, he elaborated:

"There are no 'no-growth' companies; there are only 'no-growth' managements."

To assess divisional performance, Sutton employed a set of five control mechanisms: preoperational controls, such as establishing plans, budgets, and forecasts; operational reviews; statistical reports; field visits; and organizational criticism and recommendations. But the most telling evidence of an ailing division, he maintained, emerged during the field visits. "It's all about the people running these companies that determine success," Sutton asserted. "The guy running the forklift is a litmus test of the company." On another occasion, he commented: "We'd go into a plant and

DOVER CORPORATION   FOUNDATIONS

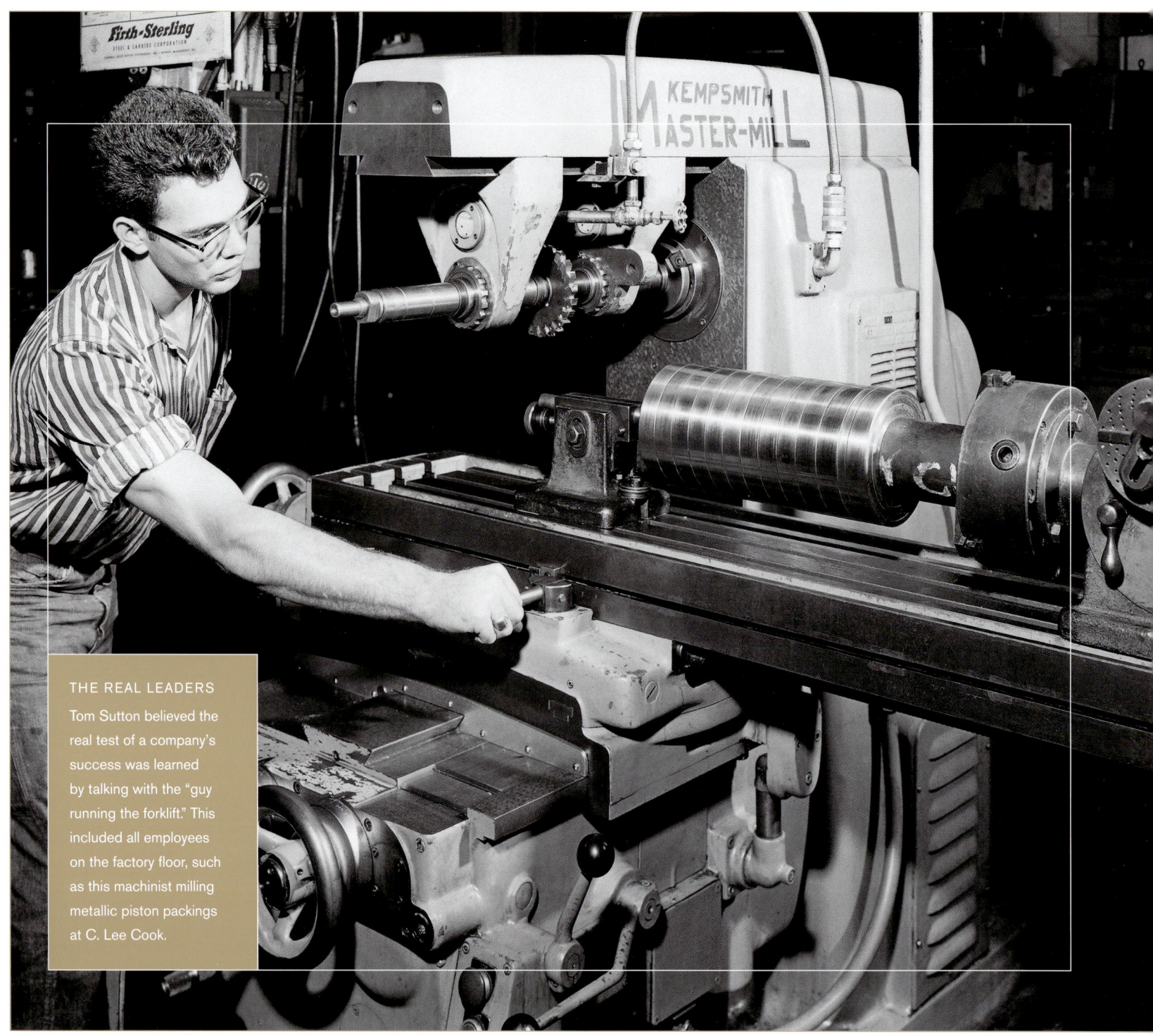

THE REAL LEADERS
Tom Sutton believed the real test of a company's success was learned by talking with the "guy running the forklift." This included all employees on the factory floor, such as this machinist milling metallic piston packings at C. Lee Cook.

INNOVATION: DE-STA-CO'S TOGGLE CLAMP

The invention of the first manual toggle clamp in 1936 by DE-STA-CO literally changed industry by offering a unique value proposition to manufacturers—the ability to eliminate threaded fasteners and thereby reduce set-up and part-to-part change-over times. DE-STA-CO originally was founded as a stamping company in 1915, but found its true calling as a maker of toggle clamps in the 1930s, a period when the Motor City reverberated with automobile companies. Having invented a viable means to reduce manufacturing time, DE-STA-CO's toggle clamp, soon found applications in other industries, such as the aviation market. In 2003, the company reinvented its signature product, giving it twice the holding capacity in the same "envelope" size as previous toggle clamps, earning the company yet another patent. Today, DE-STA-CO is to toggle clamps what Kleenex is to tissues, and the company continues to own more than 70 percent of the U.S. toggle clamp market.

meet the head of manufacturing, the shipping department, the shipping department foreman, and so on. You'd know then whether or not orders were being fulfilled properly and how many returns they were getting. And then you knew just how healthy this company really was."

The culprit for a failing division usually was its president. "When it gets down to the nut-cracking, corporate responsibility rests in the heads of the individual businesses," Sutton said, "so you had to be sure you had the right man running them. If you did, you left them alone. If you didn't, you changed them." During Sutton's tenure as CEO through 1981, he replaced several division heads, but those decisions were the exception and not the rule. "If Tom could be faulted for anything, it was for holding onto some division heads longer than he should have," Ormsby says.

But Suesser has a different perspective. "It was very important to Tom that the people running our businesses had the same integrity he had," he explains. "So he made sure before buying a company that they did. Integrity was absolutely critical. Tom often said that a division president 'should do the right things, as well as do things right.' He didn't send internal auditors as spies to look into the companies; he usually went himself to gauge things."

Dover's different way of doing things did have its detractors. Critics, for example, questioned the continuing management effectiveness of individuals who had just sold their businesses for a large sum of money. But Sutton believed a former owner's "loyalty to his employees, his sense of responsibility to his customers, his moral obligation to us, and the competitive spirit with other Dover division presidents usually make him an even better manager than before," he said. "In short, he is even less tolerant of inefficiency as a member of the team."

HOLDING FIRM
DE-STA-CO set the bar higher with the redesign of its legendary work-holding solution in 2003, developing a new manual toggle clamp, left, that offers twice the holding capacity in a smaller package than the original 1936 model and eliminates pinch points.

DOVER CORPORATION FOUNDATIONS

BULLISH ON BEARINGS

Dover acquired Waukesha Bearings in 1977, the leading supplier worldwide of fluid film bearings for industrial, utility, government, and marine applications. Today, it also includes magnetic bearings for turbomachinery used in the power generation and oil and gas industries.

By 1967, Dover's disparate businesses comprised five major markets—elevators, general industry, petroleum production, petroleum distribution, and construction. The company manufactured a variety of products, which altogether produced more than $100 million in revenue. Dover also boasted a modest international presence: W. C. Norris owned Alberta Oil Tool in Edmonton, Canada; DE-STA-CO owned a plant near Frankfurt, Germany; and OPW was building Dover International, which opened branches in the Netherlands and Tokyo the following year.

The diversity of products, markets, and geographic locations helped Dover weather the cyclical nature of some divisions. In the company's early years, for example, products for the petroleum production industry had accounted for nearly 50 percent of its sales and more than half its profits: When oil well drilling was high, sales increased sharply for W. C. Norris equipment. But by the mid-1960s, as oil well completions sputtered in the highly cyclical market, petroleum production accounted for less than 20 percent of Dover's sales. Making up the difference was the elevator division, whose sales had increased from 13 percent in Dover's first years to more than 30 percent by the mid-1960s.

In 1971, Sutton selected Tony Ormsby, who had been his executive vice president for a year, to succeed him as CEO. Ormsby, an accountant by training, had been an invaluable executive. When problems at W. C. Norris in the early 1960s had resulted in the firing of its president, Durham had appointed Ormsby its chief financial officer, and he soon developed a plan to get the division's finances in order. In 1964, Ormsby was transferred to Dover's Washington headquarters to direct Dover's Canadian elevator and petroleum product operations, assuming the titular position of Dover Canada chairman. Much to Sutton's dismay, Ormsby did not become CEO of Dover, resigning in 1972 for personal reasons. "I could not handle the travel requirements that were necessary for the job," Ormsby explains. He remained a board director of Dover until 1999.

Bryan Earles, Jr., head of Dover Elevator, was chosen to become CEO in Ormsby's stead. Earles had succeeded Hugh Allan as president of the elevator division in 1966 and had a reputation as an astute businessman. But Earles also did not become CEO: While traveling in 1974, he suffered a fatal heart attack. Few promising candidates emerged to succeed Earles, prompting Sutton to venture outside the Dover

AUTONOMY: OPW

Dover Corporation was barely six years old when it made one of its first and best acquisitions, purchasing OPW Corporation in 1961 from G. L. Ohrstrom & Associates, which had owned OPW since 1948. Based in Cincinnati, OPW has enjoyed a long, colorful history. It was founded in 1892 by two master pattern makers, Victor E. Tresise and Joseph E. Hausfeld, each of whom put up $390 to finance The Ohio Pattern Works, as they then called it. The company boasted the first tool-and-die shop in Cincinnati to make both wood and metal patterns, and was the first to have its own foundry.

The partners manufactured a range of products from grave markers to oil valves. Cleveland had become an oil boomtown after John D. Rockefeller and his Standard Oil Company had struck the mother lode, and Ohio Pattern Works began supplying the burgeoning petroleum industry with its line of oil valves. Pioneer automakers such as Henry Ford gave that industry a major boost by introducing gasoline-powered automobiles at the turn of the twentieth century. In 1904, OPW made the decision to concentrate its efforts on the expanding oil market. By 1916, when OPW was incorporated as The Ohio Pattern Works & Foundry Company, the OPW brand signified a range of products that included nozzles, valves, and couplings, which were sold to major oil companies, refineries, oil jobbers, and chemical companies.

The increasing numbers of automobiles in the 1930s spawned hundreds of service stations all across the country, and OPW's line of nozzles grew right along with them. In 1949 the company invented an automatic shut-off nozzle that stopped the flow of gasoline when the vehicle tank was full; that nozzle soon became the industry standard. OPW also began manufacturing products to handle petroleum-based fluids from the time they left the refinery until they were sold to the public. Research and development became a company focus, leading to the introduction of several new products, such as the first overfill-prevention valve, which greatly reduced the possibility of spillage.

By the 1950s, OPW products were used on tank trucks, for fuel oil delivery, for filling tank cars and trucks, and for fueling commercial and military aircraft. The company even produced an automatic tire inflator that accurately controlled inflated pressure. "Wherever gasoline, oil, jet fuel, chemicals, and other hazardous liquids are being handled, you will see OPW products," Dover Corporation's 1960 annual report stated. Dover provided OPW with capital to expand its production capacity, broaden its product line both internally and via acquisitions, and venture into numerous international markets over the years.

In the early 1980s, OPW was split into five separate operating units, which were subsequently recombined into three separate, independent companies in 1991: OPW Fueling Components, Engineered Systems, and Civacon. The latter two, along with Midland Manufacturing (acquired in 1994) and Knappco (acquired in 1995), merged in 1998 to form the OPW Fluid Transfer Group. Today, OPW Fueling Components makes and sells a range of products that includes liquid and gas fueling nozzles, fittings, valves, and tire inflation equipment; OPW Fluid Transfer Group makes and sells liquid transfer valves, liquid level-measuring devices, dry bulk conveying fittings, railroad and tank car safety valves, and other products.

TRUSTED PROVIDER

OPW is best known for its nozzles at the local service station. But the company's products also have applications in industrial and aerospace markets. Above: A mechanic refuels a jet airplane using twin OPW nozzles.

DOVER CORPORATION FOUNDATIONS

SUCKER ROD SUCCESS

The phenomenal 604 percent increase in Norris sales in 1974 encouraged the company to expand sucker rod production. By 1976 a $6 million plant was completed in Tulsa, Oklahoma, ready to supply sucker rods, above, to expectant customers.

divisions to choose an executive of Singer Corporation, Stuart Tisdale, as his executive vice president and heir apparent. As in the case of Otto Schwenk, the appointment was a mistake. Tisdale was attuned to a more controlled corporate environment and was soon released. Consequently, Sutton, like his mentor Durham, ran Dover far longer than he had anticipated, filling in as CEO several times between 1971 and 1976, when another CEO finally was appointed—and stayed in office.

In the interim, Sutton ran herd over several additional acquisitions: Davenport Machine Tool; Hammond & Champness, Dover's first British elevator operation; Ernest Holmes, a manufacturer of automotive wreckers; Louisiana Elevator; and Campbell Elevator. He also shepherded Dover through the first Arab oil embargo in 1973 and the nascent environmental movement, which stimulated stricter government regulations affecting myriad industries.

The oil embargo by the Organization of Petroleum Exporting Countries spurred domestic energy production, stimulating an astonishing 604 percent increase in sales of Norris's oil production equipment, such as sucker rods and subsurface pumps, in 1974. Norris was well prepared for the sudden spurt in demand, having acquired two new product lines in 1972. But the surging demand strained Norris's production capacity at the seams. In 1976, to ease the production constraints, Dover funded the building of a new $6 million sucker rod plant in Tulsa, as well as a $1 million addition to the subsurface oil pump plant, both slated for operation in 1977.

Norris's remarkable rebound in the 1970s generated considerable capital for Dover, which Sutton earmarked for future acquisitions. Further fueling Dover's fortunes was nozzle-maker OPW, which benefited from the trend toward self-service gas stations and the introduction of unleaded gasoline, the latter stirred by the burgeoning environmental movement. Both developments fostered the purchase of new gasoline dispensing equipment at service stations.

Despite the recessionary economy of the 1970s, caused in large part by rising fuel costs, Dover enjoyed its fourteenth and fifteenth consecutive years of increases in both sales and earnings in 1974 and 1975. Fifteen of Dover's nineteen major product lines were number one in their respective markets in 1975 or had such a unique design that no comparable product competed against them. The other four products were in the top three in their respective industries. Sutton attributed the corporation's solid performance to its singular management philosophy of strong, autonomous divisional management, lean corporate staff, high return on capital employed, strict acquisition standards, and product leadership.

Dover continued to hunt for companies suiting its acquisition criteria, which remained essentially unchanged from Ohrstrom's and Durham's initial standards. In 1975, Dieterich Standard, a market leader that owned valuable patents on devices for measuring liquid flows, squarely fit the bill. Dieterich also possessed strong management: Its president and minority owner, Gary Roubos, was a Harvard Business School graduate who had cut his teeth at forest products company Boise Cascade before hiring on at Dieterich in 1969.

When Dover came knocking with an offer to buy Dieterich, Roubos was reluctant to sell. "I was ambivalent about it, really quite content to continue running the company as it was," Roubos explains. "Cam Caswell… tried to change my mind. He said I would get a nice infusion of cash and still get to run the business the same way I had before with no interference from Dover in New York. 'That's the way all our companies operate,' Cam insisted. I said I found that hard to believe. So, Cam advised I go around and visit Dover's division presidents to erase any doubt."

Roubos met with five presidents, including Bill Petter, president of Blackmer Pump (and former president and part-owner of Ronningen-Petter); Tom Reece, the current president of Ronningen-Petter; and Bill Davidson,

GOING UP

Rotary Lift, which was one of Dover's four pillar companies, turned its elevator division into the independent Dover Elevator in 1960, after this photo of an elevator technician was taken. Both Rotary Lift and Dover Elevator continued to provide solid earnings for Dover well into the 1970s.

DOVER CORPORATION . FOUNDATIONS

AUTONOMY: UNIVERSAL

Universal Instruments, which Dover Corporation acquired in 1979, traces its roots to the Universal Instruments and Metal Company, founded in 1919 in Vestal, New York. The company was chartered to "purchase patents and manufacture implements and appliances of all kinds and descriptions." It focused initially on manufacturing metal and wire products, culminating in its debut line—"Nu-Hed" safety pins.

By 1921, Universal's backers, a group of fifty shareholders, discovered that producing and selling the popular household item was more difficult than they had anticipated. They engaged two local business consultants, who counseled Universal to abandon safety pins in favor of machining metal parts to order for local industries.

It was the right guidance: The region was fast becoming an industrial nexus, and burgeoning factories soon turned to Universal for tools, dies, and other precision parts. Close control of its costs helped Universal survive the economic depression of the 1930s and grow during World War II as the company's tool-and-die talents were pressed to meet the needs of the state's small-arms manufacturers. This work continued until the 1950s when Universal entered the short-run stamping field, making components used in collators, sorters, and other machines.

While assisting IBM in a project for the United States government, Universal's technicians were exposed to assembly problems for printed circuit boards. At that time, circuit boards were developing into compact replacements for the bulkier wiring that had connected electrical components in a computer previously, but the leaded components were still inserted into the boards by hand. IBM asked Universal's engineers and machinists to work with its designers to build a machine that could insert the components into the board.

In 1961, Universal unveiled the first semi-automatic insertion machines, which sequenced and inserted components into holes in printed circuit boards. Universal later licensed the technology and sold the equipment to other customers. The company dominated the "through-hole" component-insertion market through the 1980s; but, as technology demanded smaller and more densely populated circuit boards, new surface-mount applications were introduced that seriously competed against through-hole applications.

In 1991, *Business Week* magazine concluded that the transition to surface-mount applications spelled "deep trouble" for Universal. But the company rebounded, teaming up with Motorola, Inc., and a dozen other manufacturers and suppliers to develop a new, highly accurate factory tool for assembling components into circuit boards. By the end of the 1990s, Universal's core competencies also included component handling, prepping and centering, pinpoint part placement, systems integration, and other platform-based surface-mount technologies.

Today, Universal Instruments provides innovative circuit, semiconductor, and back-end assembly technologies and equipment, integrated system solutions, and process expertise to manufacturers in every sector of the electronics industry.

UNIVERSAL AMBITIONS

In 1979, Dover acquired Universal Instruments, a market-leading maker of electronic component insertion machines. Since that time, the company has metamorphosed into a leading manufacturer of surface-mount machines, such as the Genesis series, above.

president of W. C. Norris. "They all told me the same thing, which I found surprising," Roubos says. "Here were these people who didn't know each other well, working for this loosely managed corporation, and yet they all had the same perceptions. I thought they were colluding. But it was the truth: Freedom to 'do their own thing' was given high value."

Dover bought Dieterich Standard for $11 million in cash. Four months after the deal closed in late 1975, Sutton asked Roubos to join him in New York as his executive vice president. He had finally found Dover's next CEO. But the former flying ace still piloted the corporation for several more years until Roubos took the controls in 1981.

And what a ride it was: Dover's sales and earnings soared in the late 1970s. In 1979 Dover recorded its nineteenth consecutive year of earnings increases. Norris was the main contributor, but even smaller companies such as Rotary Lift did their share. Rotary's average annual sales were up 19 percent since 1970, and in 1977 the company reported a record 13.6 percent sales increase. That same year, the combined sales of just four Dover divisions—Rotary Lift, Norris, Dover Elevator, and C. Lee Cook—amounted to $249 million, a considerable increase from the under $20 million Dover had recorded in 1955.

The robust internal growth of many divisions fueled several late-decade acquisitions by Dover, including Waukesha Bearings, a manufacturer of specialty industrial bearings and seals, and Tranter, a producer of heat transfer and cooling equipment. Tranter made fuel-saving equipment under the Retromizer brand, which fared well during the era of energy conservation in the 1970s.

But Sutton's biggest acquisition, by far, was Universal Instruments in 1979, a company that matched some, but not all, of Dover's acquisition criteria. Although Universal had begun in 1919 as a contract tool-and-die manufacturer, it had migrated into other lines of business through the years and, by the late 1970s, was largely focused on making production equipment for the installation of components on electronic circuit boards and on selling its products to manufacturers in the computer and communications industries. The majority of Universal's business was component-insertion equipment—machines that mount leads and wires into position on printed circuit boards. In short, Universal was clearly an Information Age company—not the typical metal manufacturer that Dover usually courted.

Universal also was a public company and quite large by Dover's customary standards,

BUYING INTO TECHNOLOGY

Dover CEO Gary Roubos continued Sutton's strategy of diversifying into the technology sector to balance the volatility in the petroleum market, acquiring seven technology companies between 1979 and 1984. Below: Universal Instruments' Axial Lead Sequencer from 1983.

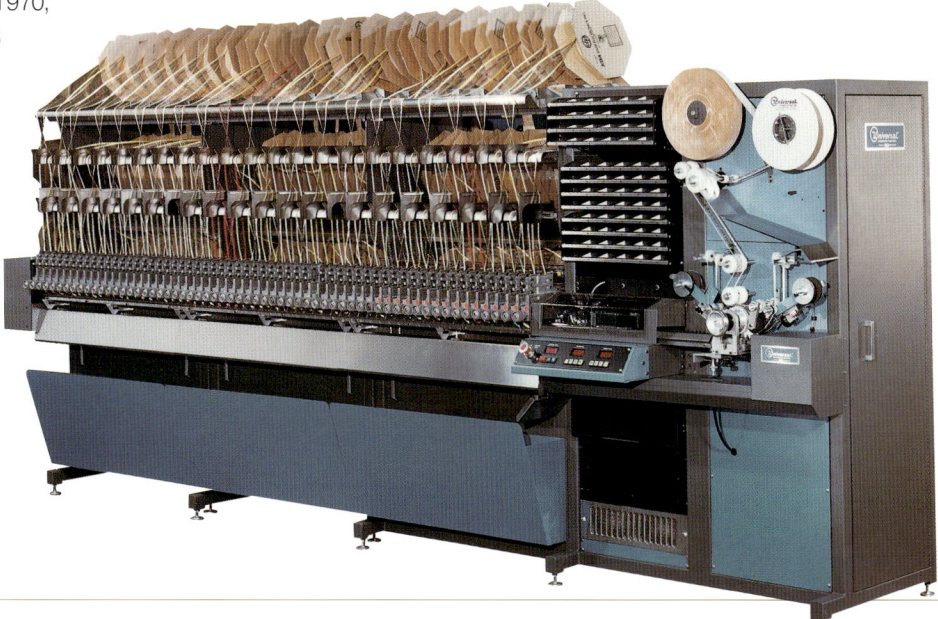

DOVER CORPORATION FOUNDATIONS

with more than 1,100 employees and a purchase price of $59 million. "There was no question when we bought Universal that we perceived it as a very different acquisition than what we had been doing previously," Roubos comments.

Universal did meet Dover's criteria for growth—a compounded annual rate of 21 percent in sales and 30 percent in earnings over the preceding ten years—and for management, particularly in its president and minority owner, Floyd "Rudy" Lawson, a former Big Ten basketball player at Purdue University and, like Sutton, a pilot, to boot. But Lawson, like Roubos before him, was less than eager to sell his company. "Once Rudy met Tom Sutton, that's all it took," says John Pomeroy, named Universal's president in 1985. "They were each other's kind of people. They trusted each other implicitly, and the deal moved forward." Universal Instruments would play an important role in Dover's sales and earnings in the 1990s, a decade of tremendous growth in the technology sector.

As the difficult economic conditions of the 1970s eased with the new decade, Dover stood a much larger company than it had been ten years earlier. Its scale of operations had increased substantially, albeit without a corresponding increase in administrative complexity or personnel at headquarters. Sutton limited central activities to publicly reporting results, monitoring the health of the divisions, and developing a portfolio of well-run, diversified businesses. As Sutton often

POWER FLOW

Gary Roubos (sitting left), succeeded Tom Sutton as Dover CEO and president in 1981. Roubos began work for Dover following the acquisition of Dieterich Standard, where he was part-owner and president.

remarked, "A mushrooming bureaucracy can hamstring corporate management."

During the 1970s, a decade of runaway inflation, Sutton had maintained the corporate model of low overhead, helping him resist the need for drastic cost-cutting measures and divestitures—the tactics of other large conglomerates to preserve cash. By conserving expenses and pursuing a conservative policy of borrowing, Sutton could take the money generated by the divisions and profitably invest it in acquisitions. All told, Sutton had spent $117 million on acquisitions between 1971 and 1980, much of it cash; yet, Dover's total debt in 1980 was only $31 million more than it had been in 1970.

As the decade of the 1980s began, few companies could boast Dover's vital statistics: a 15.5 percent annual-sales growth rate and 16.8 percent annual growth in net profits from 1964, the year Sutton became CEO, to 1980. The following year, when forty-four-year-old Gary Roubos assumed the post of chief executive, Dover announced it had joined the ranks of billion-dollar companies. Sutton, who remained chairman of the board, gave Roubos the same advice his predecessor had given him. "I told Gary, this is a good company; don't f—— it up," Sutton smiled. "I picked Gary because he understood and accepted the Dover Philosophy and wasn't about to upset the apple cart. And he didn't."

Six feet, four inches tall, a dapper, refined man with a luxuriant moustache, Roubos says the key to Dover, as he saw it, was "to pick the right people and let them continue to do well what they had been doing well. That was the thing I wanted to keep in place above all else."

Roubos's initial years at the helm were taxing. In January 1981, unemployment, inflation, and mortgage rates all were in the double digits. Foreign competition, particularly from Japanese manufacturers, carved a swath out of the automobile, electronics, and communications markets. A severe economic recession, the worst since the Great Depression, caused Dover's per-share earnings in 1982 to fall for the first time in twenty-one years. The oil equipment industry that had buoyed much of Dover's profits in the seventies took a turn for the worse as new drilling and production in the petroleum field declined amid falling fuel prices. The energy crash reverberated at W. C. Norris. Norris's sales and earnings fell in 1982 for the first time in twenty-one years. The following year's tallies were even worse—sales and earnings plunged 30 percent and 59 percent, respectively. "The industry was in free fall," recalls Tom Reece, who was appointed Norris's president in early 1983 in the midst of the downward spiral. Reece had previously headed up Ronningen-Petter and DE-STA-CO.

"We had a huge over-capacity situation, having just added to our sucker rod plant. We now had the capability to produce 125 million feet of sucker rods a year, and here we were in 1983 producing 45 to 48 million feet, with total industry demand less than 80 million feet," Reece explains. "Meanwhile, our competitors are dropping prices like crazy—customers who had felt gouged for years now had the bat in their hands. Fortunately, we were still the premier quality sucker rod manufacturer in the world. But there were no silver bullets. Only good, hard grunt work through the remainder of the decade would get us back on track."

There were some bright spots during the decade, including robust sales at both Rotary Lift and DE-STA-CO. Declining fuel prices increased automobile usage and production, boosting Rotary Lift to record sales and earnings in 1983. The surge in automobile production

DOVER CORPORATION FOUNDATIONS

PACKING UP

Tipper Tie, which Dover acquired in 1981, manufactures innovative packaging closure systems. Founded in 1952, the company's second-tie machine, the Tipper Clipper, being used right and shown below, used U-shaped aluminum wire clips to hold meat casings closed for processing.

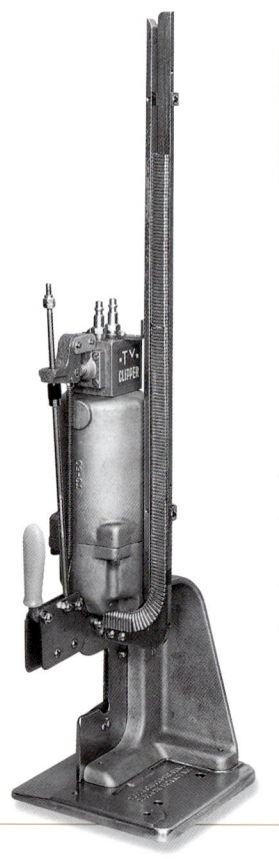

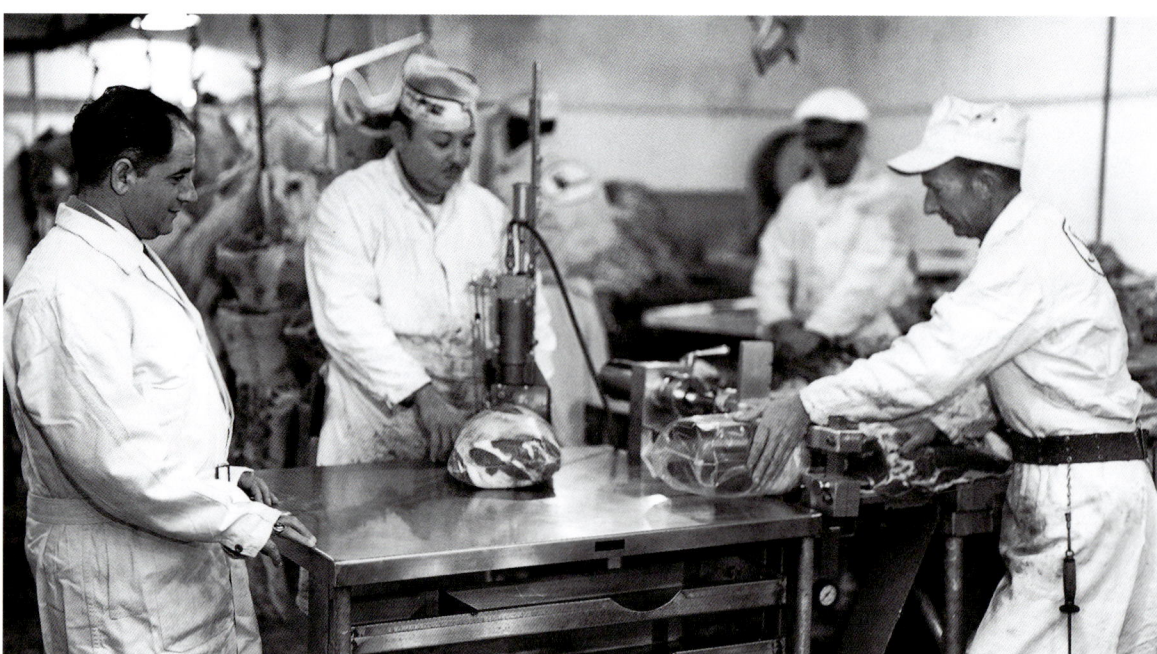

in the United States, coupled with new housing starts, also lifted DE-STA-CO's earnings substantially in 1983 and 1984. Again, Dover's inherent diversification was a cushion.

Roubos relied on the presidents of the Dover divisions to guide their companies capably through the recession, liberating him to focus on growing the corporation. Three new corporate officers eventually assisted him: Edward Kata, an acquisitions specialist who replaced Cam Caswell upon his retirement in 1981; John Brant, formerly the head of the elevator division, who became Roubos's executive vice president also in 1981; and John McNiff, recruited in 1983 as Bob Bethe neared retirement.

Roubos's first acquisition, in 1981, was Tipper Tie, a maker of precision metal clip closures used for packing meats and dairy and poultry products. But, after a lull in 1982, Dover acquired six more companies in 1983, among them K&L Microwave, a manufacturer of radio-frequency microwave filters and systems; DEK Printing Machines, which makes screen printers for hybrid and printed circuit boards; and Soltec, producer of automated soldering and cleaning systems for assembled, printed circuit boards. The latter two not only complemented Universal Instruments' product lines; they were headquartered in Europe—DEK in the United Kingdom and Soltec in the Netherlands—giving Dover a wider international footprint.

Roubos's early acquisition strategy focused predominantly on the rapidly growing technology sector, which he perceived vital to balancing dwindling revenues coming from the petroleum industry. Between 1979 and 1984, Dover acquired seven technology companies, of which five were in the 1983–1984 time frame alone. Taking his cue from the successful development of Dover's elevator division, Roubos created a new electronics products subsidiary in 1984, composed of the recently acquired, complementary technology companies.

In 1984, Dover also made its biggest and most expensive acquisition to date, spending $75.3 million to buy Sargent Industries, a public company that supplied specialized components to defense-related businesses. Like Universal Instruments, Sargent fit some but not all traditional Dover acquisition criteria. It enjoyed pretax earnings of nearly 15 percent on sales, and its divisions sold niche products to military and industrial companies, with the United States government its top customer. But Sargent comprised seven separate enterprises that were operated with more centralized controls than was common at other Dover companies. Moreover, some but not all of its products, such as rocket motor cases, hydraulic controls for submarines, and aircraft cockpit controls, were not market leaders and were subject to volatile government contract funding. And its CEO wanted to retire upon acquisition.

Initially, Dover had declined to buy Sargent, believing the price too high, but, when Sargent lowered the price, Dover took the plunge. "We felt that Sargent, at a time when foreign competition was bruising us, at least contracted with a customer that would not be affected by foreign competition—the U.S. government," Roubos explains. Nevertheless, the Sargent acquisition would prove problematic in the ensuing years, requiring both leadership changes and substantial reorganization. The company would reemerge a highly successful enterprise in the 1990s and on into the next decade.

By 1984, the economy had sprung back to life, and "stagflation," the combination of high inflation and high unemployment, had finally disappeared. To revive the economy, President Ronald Reagan supported tighter money policies at the United States Federal Reserve and stepped up the pace of deregulation, especially in the energy sector. He also forced through sweeping reductions in marginal income tax rates and then indexed those rates for inflation.

But in the mid-eighties, the sheer size of Dover rendered central oversight daunting for the New York office despite its exercise of traditional minimum controls. The scale of Dover had become enormous compared to the nugget of small companies that had formed the original corporation in 1955. The corporation of the eighties listed thirty-four divisions, seventeen of them added between 1979 and 1984. Meanwhile, eight of the seventeen presidents of the pre-1979 Dover divisions had retired or resigned, creating a situation in which many divisions now had new leadership at the helm. Roubos was not about to fiddle with the dyed-in-the-wool Dover principle of divisional autonomy—he once told a magazine reporter that being the president of a

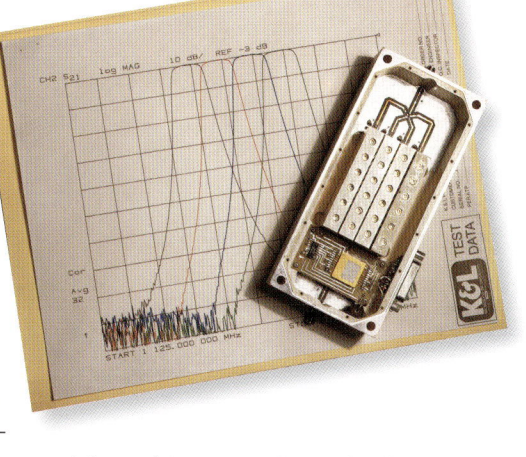

CLEANSING THE AIRWAVES

Dover acquired K&L Microwave, a maker of radio-frequency microwave filters, in 1983. Purchased during a difficult economic time, the company survived and has grown to produce such high-tech devices as this filter.

MILITARY SERVICE

Sargent Controls & Aerospace has manufactured precision control components for air, water, and land vehicles since the 1960s. Sargent first entered the aerospace business during World War II, designing components for airplanes, such as cockpit gears.

UHF
OFF
MAIN
BOTH
ADF
VOL
PRESET
MANUAL
GUARD
TONE
OFF ON
SQUELCH
DOWNLOCK OVERRIDE
L/G WRN SILENCE
FUEL
MILES
COURSE
CLIMB
YAW DAMPER
CONT

DOVER CORPORATION   FOUNDATIONS

INNOVATION: SARGENT'S QUIET TECHNOLOGY

In 1969 Sargent Controls and Aerospace won the bid to begin development work on the crucial quiet control valve technology for the United States Navy submarine program. At the time, the government was concerned about Navy submarines putting out a sonic "signature" when being hunted, and it turned to Sargent and other manufacturers to make the quietest possible marine valves to raise and lower torpedoes into tubes for deployment. Sargent earned the coveted contract to begin engineering work for a prototype hydraulic control valve on the Trident and SSN-688 Class nuclear powered submarines. Thanks to its efforts, the U.S. Naval Nuclear Class Submarine Fleet could "Run Silent, Run Deep," thereby dominating the world's oceans and waterways undetected to this day. Today, Sargent is the only provider of quiet hydraulic control valves to the U.S. Navy and its reinvigorated Seawolf-class submarine program.

Dover company was "the next best thing to owning your own"—but he realized the necessity of organizational restructuring. "We just couldn't be in close contact with all those divisions the current way we were structured," Roubos explains.

His first effort was to appoint his executive vice president, John Brant, as CEO of the new electronics products group. Brant had experience in overseeing the various companies that constituted Dover Elevator. "But John, much to our surprise, got an offer from another company and left us somewhat in the lurch," Roubos notes. "So, we named Rudy Lawson, who headed Universal Instruments, as this subsidiary's head. It became, in essence, a clone of Dover." The new subsidiary was called Dover Technologies.

Roubos then appointed Rotary Lift president Dick Farrell to replace Brant as executive vice president and put him in charge of monitoring the remaining divisions. The task proved impossible. "It damn near killed Dick,"

Roubos says. "It was such a huge load, and I realized I could not have one guy do all this. It was just not possible. So we pushed the discussion and debate out to the divisions at a meeting in the Caribbean. And, gradually, it became clear that the Dover clone we had essentially created with the technology group, and before that the elevator company, could be duplicated with the remaining companies."

In 1985, that strategy was undertaken. Three new subsidiaries were formed to join Dover Technologies and Dover Elevator: Dover Sargent (soon changed to Dover Diversified), Dover Resources, and Dover Industries. Each super-subsidiary, as they were then called, boasted its own CEO, all of them culled from the ranks of Dover divisions: Tom Reece became head of Dover Resources; Lew Burns, Dover Industries; Rudy Lawson, Dover Technologies; John Apple, Dover Elevator; and Jerry Yochum, Dover Diversified. Their jobs were to make acquisitions, hire and fire division presidents, and monitor companies

FAR AND WIDE

Dover reorganized into five subsidiaries in the mid-1980s to monitor its growing companies more easily. Among them was C. Lee Cook, which operated the compressor valve manufacturer Cook Manley, whose busy factory floor is shown here.

DOVER CORPORATION FOUNDATIONS

under their respective authority with the same respect for independence and autonomy that had existed between Dover corporate and operating companies in the past: They exercised the same authority over investment proposals, personnel selection, compensation, and business plans that Dover's CEOs had traditionally exercised.

Even Fred Durham, from his farm in Virginia, had some say in the restructuring of Dover. In a handwritten letter to Roubos in 1985, eighty-six-year-old Durham wrote: "If the super-sub is to clone Dover, then the super-sub office should stand in the same relationship as the New York office stands with OPW." Durham's counsel was heeded.

The divisions, renamed operating companies, would retain their independence but henceforward would report to the appropriate subsidiary CEO. The challenge then was to divide them up in an effective manner. Dover Elevator and Dover Technologies each comprised complementary companies, and Dover Diversified represented six of the seven companies that Sargent Industries had encompassed at the time of its acquisition. The rest of the operating companies were diverse in product lines, market, and geographic locations. "Gary, Tom Reece, and I met in my office near O'Hare Airport in Chicago and split them up," recalls Lew Burns, Dover Industries' CEO.

"There was no consideration given to industry; it was more like Gary would retain oversight of some

THE NEXT GENERATION

Dover's executive staff, officers, and company presidents gather for an official portrait in 1984, the year the new subsidiary structure was announced. In the front row are CEO and president Gary Roubos, left, and Tom Sutton, right.

companies for a period of time, and Tom and I would split up the rest. There were certain presidents Gary wanted to work with and companies that I was familiar with and Tom was familiar with. There was some consideration given to geography. For example, three of the companies Reece took were in Michigan. But there was no grand strategic vision, and that was fine. Dover, after all, had existed successfully for years with no synergy in terms of the companies that comprised it."

Under the new subsidiary structure, the five subsidiary CEOs were granted the authority to make acquisitions of stand-alone companies within certain financial parameters and concurrent with analytical input from New York. Burns, for example, would spend more than $1 billion on acquisitions over the next fifteen years as he built Dover Industries. "My job was to oversee this portfolio of companies, take the cash they generated, and do acquisitions," he says.

The subsidiary CEOs would manage their mini-Dovers as if managing separate, independent public companies. Fortunately, they had as their guide the historic paradigm of Dover and the leadership principles set forth by Durham and, especially, Sutton.

It is perhaps fitting that on January 1, 1986, when Sutton retired as an officer and employee of the corporation after more than twenty years service at corporate headquarters, Dover's financial health was at its peak. In 1963, the year before he had become president, Dover had had sales of $68 million and net earnings of $4 million. By 1985, sales and earnings had grown more than twenty-fold to $1.4 billion and $100 million, respectively. Stockholder equity had grown, even faster, from $23 million to $625 million. Perhaps the most telling evidence of Sutton's impact was the value of a single share of Dover stock in 1985: Not counting dividends, which increased every year, it had grown more than thirty-fold since he had taken the helm at Dover.

Sutton did not create the Dover Philosophy, which had already become deeply rooted when he arrived at corporate headquarters. But he nurtured and cultivated it in a new generation of managers. The company was on solid footing. Now those managers stepped forward to build upon the foundation.

REORGANIZATION

Dover's 1985 first quarter report, left, commented on the historic management reorganization, affirming that the new structure "will enable us to preserve the entrepreneurial spirit that has been so instrumental in Dover's success."

CLEANING UP In 1993, Dover acquired Heil Company, a maker of refuse collection vehicle bodies, founded in 1901. Initially, Heil was in the business of welding rails together, a novel process that had replaced the customary method of securing rails with wire. In 1919, Heil started making dump body hoists pulled by teams of horses—its entrée into the refuse collection business. Through the years, Heil Environmental Industries, as it is now called, has unveiled numerous innovative products, such as the Python, above, which boasts the most technically advanced, automated arm in a side-loading refuse collection vehicle. Like many Dover operating companies, Heil has successfully incorporated sophisticated technology into traditional manufacturing.

2 TILT TOWARD GROWTH

The restructured Dover Corporation in January 1986 comprised thirty-seven operating companies, thirty-three of them reporting to the chief executive officers of the five new subsidiaries, and four reporting to Dover's corporate office. The subsidiary CEOs were responsible for maintaining close relationships with each of their operating company presidents and for being intimately knowledgeable about each president's plans, prospects, and performance. As Tom Reece, a former Dover Resources CEO, comments, "The system works when we have a capable, dedicated operating company president who assumes ownership of his company and responsibility for all the company's actions and results. My job was to be sure the right person was in place."

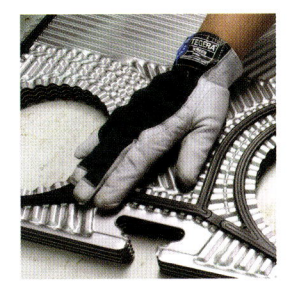

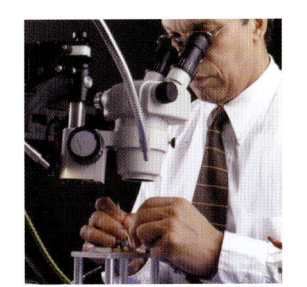

UNIVERSAL GAINS

Dover was buoyed through much of the 1980s by the booming business of Dover Technologies. Universal Instruments, in particular, enjoyed robust growth. During this time, the company's full assembly floor was always alive with orders and employees.

M E A
DIP AREA

DOVER CORPORATION   TILT TOWARD GROWTH

HQ TAKES A BREAK
Under Roubos, the Dover head office stepped back from orchestrating acquisitions and instituted a five-subsidiary structure, with subsidiary CEOs heading acquisitions of new operating companies. Below: A relaxed Gary Roubos, pictured in Antigua during a Dover-organized executive retreat, where the new subsidiary structure was announced to Dover operating company presidents.

Like all publicly traded corporations, Dover has a fiduciary duty to shareholders to build long-term value and provide an attractive return on equity. To generate value and growth, each of the five subsidiaries was deemed a base upon which to add other companies through acquisitions. The acquisition criteria remained the same: Candidates must be profitable companies that had high return on investment, were leaders in their markets, and had a niche or proprietary product in industries that Dover understood, and had capable leaders willing to stay after Dover Corporation acquired their companies. What would change was that, rather than one Dover Corporation engineering all acquisitions, five mini-Dovers would negotiate acquisitions, observing the same value-investing as had Dover's corporate office in the past.

A fundamental tenet of the new subsidiary structure was the empowerment of subsidiary CEOs to make acquisitions. But delivering on that promise was complicated. For one thing, Gary Roubos and Dover's board of directors were at first concerned by the subsidiary CEOs' relative lack of expertise in discerning viable acquisition candidates and negotiating the deals. "Initially, the guys running the subsidiaries were primarily involved with the operations of the companies under their oversight and not so much with acquisitions, which were still handled by New York," Roubos recalls. "What we had to do was to take these fellows now running the subsidiaries and train them how to do acquisitions. They had no experience, and we had a lot of experience."

Accordingly, in the early years of the new subsidiary structure, acquisition authority was meted out sparingly. Subsidiary CEOs grumbled that Dover's corporate office, in the guise of acquisitions specialist Ed Kata, continued to scout out promising candidates and handle most of the negotiations. "Ed would go out and look for acquisitions, handle the bidding, develop the handshake with the seller, and we had to step back through this whole process and be the support person," says Dover Industries CEO Lewis Burns. "It took a while to convince Gary [Roubos] that we needed to conduct the negotiations. If we didn't, then we would not develop the close relations with the seller—the managements that in most cases would continue running these companies—that we needed. If Dover New York bought a company and simply passed it off to us, there would be a different chemistry at play. Gradually, Gary saw our side of things, and we gained more authority to make these deals."

Putting the CEOs squarely in charge of acquisitions would serve a stated purpose of the subsidiary structure: to prepare the subsidiaries for the possibility of standing alone as independent public companies, were that deemed to be in the best interests of Dover's shareholders. "Gary said, 'Look, your job is to be ready to go public if it is to the stockholders' advantage,'" Burns recalls. "He truly believed that the subsidiaries would be worth more to stockholders as five separate entities rather than one Dover. However, we CEOs did not necessarily drive our subsidiaries in that direction. One thing different about Dover versus other corporations is that we have very modest egos here. We're very loyal to building stockholder value but felt, if we could build this value and remain a part of Dover, that was our preference."

The subsidiary CEOs were a collegial group of like-minded men, sitting on each other's boards of directors and sharing an unshakable conviction in Dover's business model, each having experienced it firsthand as the former president of a successful operating company. Each had a different leadership style, based upon their dissimilar personalities. Some favored more laissez-faire dealings with company presidents, and others preferred more personal interactions. Burns, for instance, often encouraged the presidents of Dover Industries' companies to gather together in meetings without him or other subsidiary board members present. Jerry Yochum, CEO of Dover Sargent (later Dover Diversified) and the former president of Waukesha Bearings, brought yet a different style, since many of his businesses were troubled at that time.

John Pomeroy, who succeeded Rudy Lawson as CEO of Dover Technologies in 1987, was accommodating of operating companies faring well but was more hands-on with those not performing up to snuff. Reece at Dover Resources employed Sutton's Socratic method of personally visiting operating companies and asking questions of managers, "questions that embodied the answers," Reece winks. And John Apple, CEO of Dover Elevator, essentially presided over the most vertical subsidiary within Dover, in which company executives knew each other's businesses thoroughly and were attuned to working together closely.

IN FIRM HANDS

Dover's leadership team in the late 1980s consisted of CEO Gary Roubos (seated, front), Dover executives, and the subsidiary CEOs, who monitored the financial performance of their constituent operating companies from regionally located offices.

DOVER CORPORATION   TILT TOWARD GROWTH

THE FINANCE TEAM

Monitoring the combined health of Dover's subsidiaries and constituent companies through much of the 1980s and 1990s were Fred Suesser (left), Dover controller who joined the corporation in 1962, and John McNiff (right), formerly Dover's treasurer and later its chief financial officer.

Although their leadership styles differed, the CEOs were unified on the principle of operating company independence. "We believe that the Dover Philosophy is the right way to run a business and will passionately work to that end," Pomeroy says. Burns concurs: "We would never do anything to interfere with a president feeling total ownership and accountability."

To obtain a unified view of operations to ensure that the corporation functioned as a cohesive whole, Dover established a system of formal and informal executive summits. Each subsidiary CEO gathered formally with Dover's corporate officers at least once a year at the subsidiary CEO meeting in New York, where they shared ideas and best practices, offered insight on promising acquisition candidates, and discussed market or management problems at the companies under their care. Similarly, Dover's finance staff in New York, including CFO John McNiff and controller Fred Suesser, met annually with the finance staffs of the five subsidiaries.

"Instead of dealing with the finance person at OPW, I now dealt with the finance person at Dover Resources," Suesser says. "It was that person's job now to deal with the finance people at the operating companies in that subsidiary. This was a far more effective strategy."

The subsidiary CEOs and Dover's corporate officers in New York also gathered casually and quite informally at Dover's annual quail hunting ritual at Riverview Plantation in Camilla, Georgia, a tradition that began with Fred Durham and continues to the present. Frequently, the hunting party also included various operating company presidents, all wearing appropriate gear and expected to slog through the marshes. Durham and Sutton believed a man's character was revealed "while flushing a covey of stubborn holding quail," a participant on one of those excursions commented.

As for the subsidiary CEOs' interactions with Roubos, Reece had this perspective: "It was not a superior-subordinate relationship. It was a relationship where I, as the chief executive of Dover Resources, would communicate with the person who represented the ownership of a hundred percent of our stock. I felt it important to keep Gary informed, with no surprises, at levels I believed a shareholder would be interested in. I didn't feel compelled to tell him when I would be in the office, on vacation, or what I was doing day in and day out. And I wanted the company presidents of Dover Resources to feel the same way when it came to their relationships with me."

The operating company presidents also had the occasion to meet with each other at their respective subsidiaries' annual meetings. In May 1987, Dover provided another opportunity to gather, instituting a biannual meeting of all the operating company presidents at the Gold Canyon Ranch in Apache Junction, Arizona. "There was some concern back then that the subsidiary arrangement would cause the presidents of the operating companies to lose their association with Dover," says Reece. "We felt there ought to be a way for the presidents from across the five subsidiaries to gather periodically to get to know each other and share best practices."

At those meetings, company presidents were invited to make presentations voluntarily on a particular strategy or campaign they had undertaken at their companies that might be germane to other company presidents. Additionally, a small group of presidents might form a committee to address an issue such as lean manufacturing, or an outside consultant might be brought in to give a talk on a particular subject. "We've had economists, inspirational speakers, and even magicians—whatever strikes our fancy," Reece says. "This has been an important concept that has been meaningful for Dover in terms of generating a common bond and culture among this group of fiercely autonomous people."

Those various interactions provided a means of exchange between Dover's corporate office and the subsidiaries and operating companies to discuss company performance, especially as it related to the corporation's rigorous annual targets: 25 percent after-tax return on total capital; 15 percent pretax profit margin; and 10 percent pretax income growth. Not all operating companies would meet the exacting standards each year, but most did well enough to fuel Dover's progress.

To encourage the subsidiaries and operating companies to drive longer-term value through a combination of acquisitions and internal growth, Roubos launched a new long-term incentive compensation plan linking executive cash and stock option bonuses to a matrix developed by his finance staff. The matrix featured two axes, each charting the performance of a different variable. One axis measured the average annual percentage growth of an operating company's pretax earnings over a three-year span. The other axis measured the after-tax return on invested capital in the operating company over

TAKING AIM

Hunting at Riverview, as the above painting is entitled, is an annual event for Dover corporate officers and subsidiary CEOs. Sutton (left) takes aim at a quail, while Durham (middle) waits his turn.

DOVER CORPORATION   TILT TOWARD GROWTH

LIFT CAPABILITY

In 1988, Dover acquired Texas Hydraulics, a manufacturer of hydraulic cylinders and fluid power components. Dover's capital has helped Texas Hydraulics invest in several state-of-the-art plants and high-production welding equipment like that shown here.

the three years' duration. Both axes needed to perform well for an executive to receive an optimum payout, since the high performance of just one axis would not provide the robust, long-term growth Dover needed to reward shareholders for their investment in the corporation.

The matrix created greater financial incentive for subsidiary CEOs to make stand-alone acquisitions and for company presidents to increase their companies' growth through both internal product/market development initiatives and add-on acquisitions. "Some years, the matrix paid off very handsomely and people did well," says Roubos. "We also had a number of companies over the years whose presidents got nothing."

The authority given the subsidiaries and operating companies to make acquisitions, coupled with the financial incentive provided by the compensation matrix, accelerated the pace of acquisitions in the late 1980s. Several operating companies, such as OPW and C. Lee Cook, began acquiring companies in closely related businesses that broadened their product lines, provided access to new markets and geographic territories, or added new services. Although the operating company presidents were empowered to make add-on acquisitions, their respective subsidiary CEOs ensured that the presidents met Dover's stringent acquisition criteria, and they provided analytical input where needed.

From 1984 through 1987, the corporation completed an unparalleled twenty acquisitions. Nine companies were acquired in 1986 and another six in 1988, among them Chief Automotive Systems, a maker of vehicle collision repair and measuring equipment that, at $125 million, was Dover's largest acquisition at that time. Also acquired that year was Texas Hydraulics, a manufacturer of specialty hydraulic cylinders. By and large, the twenty new companies conformed to the Dover model of being owner-managed and profitable and performing at a high level; making highly engineered, predominantly proprietary products; being simple-to-understand businesses; having limited, well-defined industrial markets; and having a leading market share—or close to it. In 1987, twenty-seven of the corporation's forty-five operating companies were number one in terms of market share, five were number two, and four were number three.

When the subsidiaries and operating companies could not find promising acquisition candidates in a given year, cash inevitably built up at the corporation, compelling Roubos to initiate a

HIGH-TECH REPAIR

For thirty years, Chief Automotive Systems, acquired by Dover in 1988, has been the leading manufacturer of collision repair products. The company's product lines include the electronic frame measuring system, below, which allows technicians to scan and measure vehicle damage.

DOVER CORPORATION TILT TOWARD GROWTH

AUTONOMY: QUIET STRENGTH

When Dover acquired Sargent Industries in 1984, the corporation thought it was acquiring a Dover-like entity. Sargent was a collection of seven separate divisions manufacturing precision-engineered components and specialized energy-control devices used in submarines, aircraft, and industrial and nuclear applications. The divisions all were stand-alone operations purported to be successful market leaders. But as Dover soon learned, not all of the divisions were financially healthy, and the company would require major leadership changes and divisional reorganization over the succeeding years. In short, Sargent Industries was not at all Dover-like.

Today, Sargent Controls & Aerospace, as the company is now called, is a standout Dover performer. By divesting underperforming divisions, reinvigorating its major product lines, and acquiring several synergistic companies, Sargent has recaptured its former standing as a company with a proud history. "This is a very strong company, one that has not been afraid to relinquish the legacy of the past to grasp a new future," says Jerry Yochum, CEO of Dover Diversified.

Dover Diversified is the name given the former Dover Sargent, one of the five subsidiaries formed as part of the corporation's restructuring in the mid-1980s. Initially, Dover had believed Sargent's multidivisional makeup made it a strong candidate to stand as a separate Dover subsidiary, much like Dover Technologies and Dover Elevator. But, unlike traditional Dover companies, the constituent parts of Sargent had difficulty working independently. By 1989, it was clear that four Sargent divisions had failed to meet the corporation's growth criteria. They were liquidated, and the remaining three divisions were moved to new manufacturing facilities in Tucson, Arizona, where Sargent is headquartered today.

The company was founded in 1920 by Sumner Benedict Sargent, who had obtained a patent for the design of a specialty tool for the oil tool industry. Sargent soon sold the rights to his patent to generate capital to start his own company, which supplied the oil patch with components for sucker rods and down-hole pumps. It was not until 1935 that Sargent broadened beyond the oil industry to engage the aircraft market, which remains one of its primary markets.

The company distinguished itself during World War II by supplying hydraulic valves, actuators, and other components to the military for such aircraft as the B-25 Bomber; after the war ended, it began to serve the commercial aircraft industry worldwide. In 1952, Sargent undertook research and development on a line of marine valves and actuators for nuclear powered United States Navy submarines. This line of work culminated in the creation of the company's "quiet valve" technology for the U.S. Navy in 1969. "The Navy was concerned about submarines putting out a 'signature' sound when being hunted, and they turned to Sargent to make the quietest possible marine valves to raise and lower torpedoes into the tubes," explains former Dover CEO, Tom Reece.

As the Cold War thawed in the early 1990s, military spending dropped considerably, causing yet another strategic restructuring of Sargent. The remaining parts of Sargent were consolidated into what is now known as Sargent Controls & Aerospace.

Today, Sargent Controls & Aerospace is what it had purported to be in 1984—a successful multidivisional platform company poised for further growth in the years ahead.

20,000 LEAGUES UNDER
Sargent's precision-engineered products and specialized energy-control devices are found on land, in the air, and even under water. Sargent outfits submarines, such as the above U.S. Navy Los Angeles-class vessels.

"INITIALLY, THE GUYS RUNNING THE SUBSIDIARIES WERE PRIMARILY INVOLVED WITH THE OPERATIONS OF COMPANIES . . . AND NOT SO MUCH WITH ACQUISITIONS. WHAT WE HAD TO DO WAS TO TAKE THESE FELLOWS NOW RUNNING THE SUBSIDIARIES AND TRAIN THEM HOW TO DO ACQUISITIONS."

— Gary Roubos, Dover CEO (1981–1993)

new practice—investing in Dover stock. "We see that as a good investment when we don't have other good investments," he explained.

During that same period, some companies were divested, such as Ernest Holmes in 1987, although the corporation "remained a reluctant seller at this time," Roubos says. "Frankly, we didn't have any companies that were in real trouble to the point where we didn't think they couldn't do well."

Nevertheless, some subsidiary CEOs confronted formidable challenges. At Dover Resources, Tom Reece grappled with depressed conditions in the oil industry, which had caused earnings in Dover's petroleum segment to fall by nearly half in 1986. To focus W. C. Norris more effectively on its different market segments, Reece broke the company up into five separate entities, each with its own president. Jerry Yochum at Dover Diversified had his own troubles, caused in large part by a steep decline in government bookings at the various Sargent companies. He took the opposite tack, paring the six remaining Sargent companies down to three. "I envied some of my colleagues like Lew Burns who was out there acquiring companies left and right," says Yochum. "But I was distracted by having to fix these problems first." Yochum would not make an acquisition until 1992.

One subsidiary's dour prospects often were balanced for Dover Corporation by another subsidiary's more hopeful forecast. Dover Technologies, for example, was on a roll that would not slow down until the new millennium, thanks in large part to brisk business at Universal Instruments. Universal dominated the market for through-hole equipment to insert components into printed circuit boards, the base upon which computer circuits

TIGHT SEAL

Sargent's Airtomic business unit designs and manufactures seal rings and devices for the aerospace industry. Left: A machining process used to manufacture Airtomic seal rings.

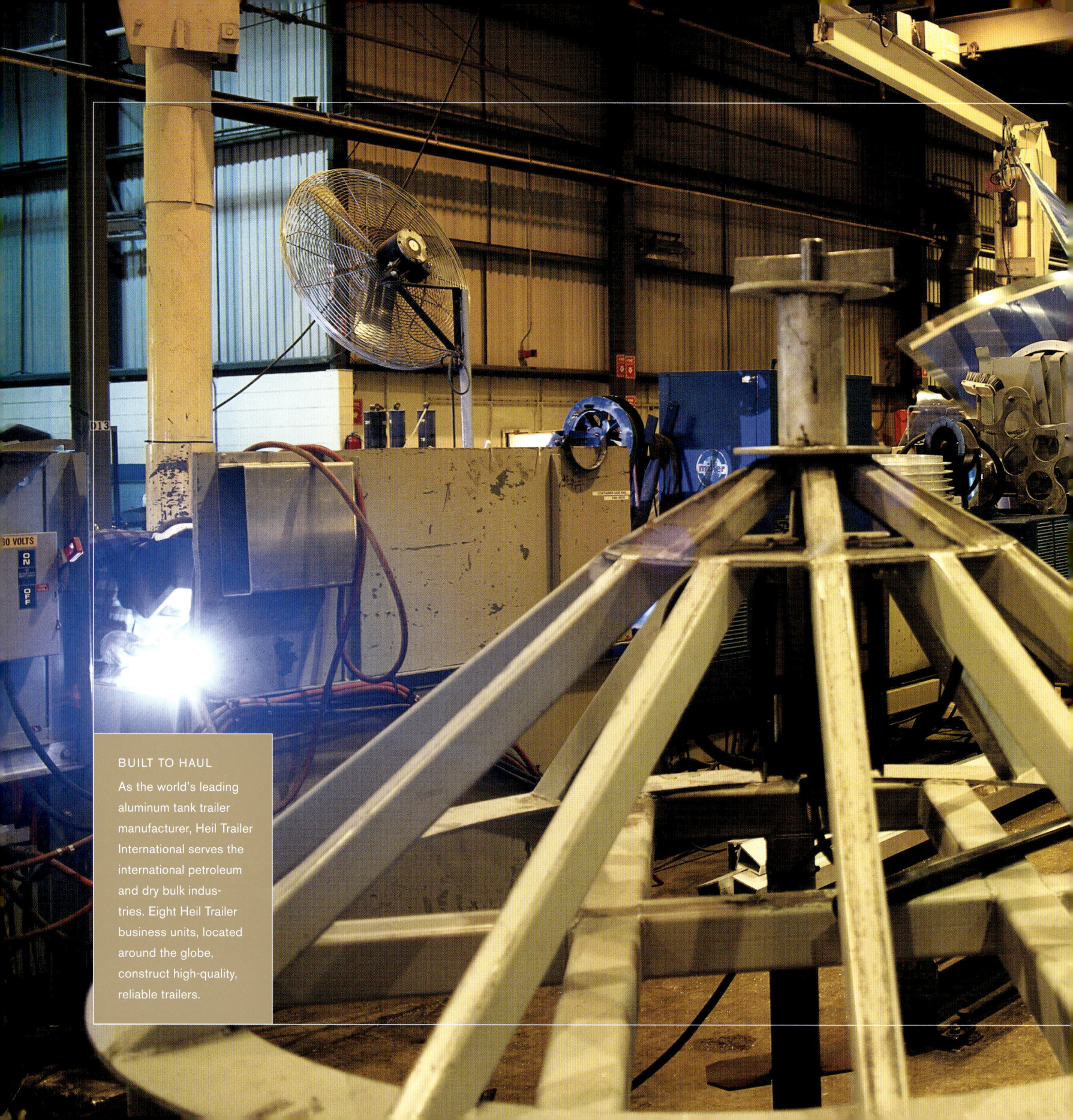

BUILT TO HAUL
As the world's leading aluminum tank trailer manufacturer, Heil Trailer International serves the international petroleum and dry bulk industries. Eight Heil Trailer business units, located around the globe, construct high-quality, reliable trailers.

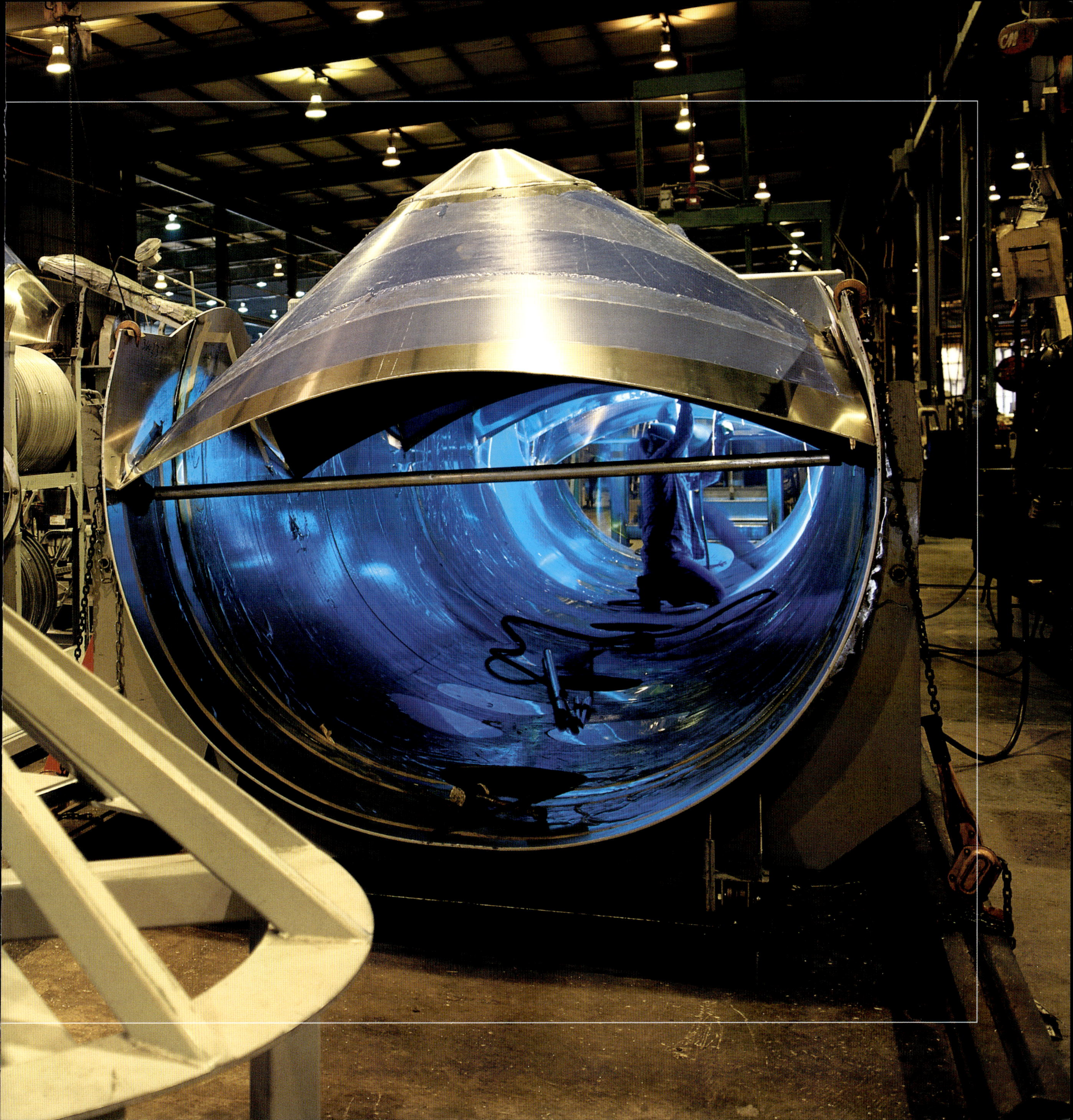

DOVER CORPORATION TILT TOWARD GROWTH

DOLLARS FOR TRASH

The horizontal baler, above, is just one example of Marathon Equipment's extensive waste-handling equipment line. The company was one of only two Dover acquisitions made during the late 1980s environment of competitive, highly leveraged company buyouts.

are printed and components are mounted. Universal's sales in 1985 were half that of 1984, but the company rebounded in 1987 to assist a 150 percent increase in profits at Dover's electronics products segment.

In 1989, Dover's corporate office, relocated to 280 Park Avenue, officially abandoned the practice of reporting its earnings by market segments—petroleum industry, building industry, electronics products, and industrial and aerospace products—and began reporting the earnings by subsidiary. The import of the decision was obvious: The subsidiary structure was then four years old, and the subsidiary CEOs had accumulated the experience to lead their units effectively as separate public companies.

The United States economy was surging in the late 1980s, and Dover rose with it. From the trough of the 1982 recession to the end of the decade, the corporation's average stock price bettered both the Standard & Poor's 500 index and the blue chips of the Dow Jones Industrial Average, an amazing accomplishment for a company whose head office staff totaled only twenty-one full-time employees and whose subsidiary staffs averaged four to five people each. Over the course of the 1980s, Dover's assets increased by nearly 300 percent, and its sales rose at an annual compounded rate of 12.26 percent to top $2 billion for the first time in 1989. Much of the growth over the decade derived from acquisitions—thirty-nine in all—for which Dover paid more than $626 million.

The business world changed dramatically as the 1980s breathed its last breath. Dover encountered stiffer competition in the acquisitions arena as investors targeted small- and medium-sized manufacturers willing to participate in highly leveraged buyouts of their

INNOVATION: UNIVERSAL'S LIGHTNING TECHNOLOGY

Universal Instruments recently unveiled the circuit board industry's fastest non-turret placement head technology, aptly named Lightning. The company's goal with Lightning, its new, modular, high-speed chip placement solution, was to combine best-in-class performance with a competitive price, as well as significantly reduce maintenance. Universal succeeded in its objectives: Lightning accurately places chips at the highest speed possible to date, via Universal's patented Variable Reluctance Motor technology. The new head features a radial array of thirty modular, individually controlled spindles, a unique configuration that delivers drive placement rates up to 54,000 components per hour for Universal's Genesis platform systems, and 30,000 components per hour for its AdVantis platform systems. Its various innovations helped Lightning win the Apex 2004 Innovation Technology Showcase award recognizing a breakthrough technology that delivers real-world benefits.

companies. The corporation failed to make a single acquisition in 1989, compelling Roubos to invest nearly $100 million dollars in Dover stock. The following year, Dover purchased another $80 million of its own stock. The corporation completed only two acquisitions in 1990, including Marathon Equipment, a manufacturer of waste compactors, conveyors, and recycling equipment.

As acquisition activity waned, Dover turned inward to spur further growth. Capital was directed to the operating companies to assist them in reengineering their internal processes to increase productivity and reduce costs, thus widening profit margins and gaining additional market share. New "lean" manufacturing systems, many borrowed from Japanese automotive manufacturers, were established at numerous Dover companies, including OPW, Blackmer Pump, and Rotary Lift, in the late 1980s. The new strategies—just-in-time manufacturing, focused factories, flow manufacturing, and cycle-time reduction—were predicated on the elimination of waste. With just-in-time manufacturing, for example, items only move through the production system as they are needed.

The reengineering efforts by Dover companies fostered a 3 percent decline in the corporation's overall inventory-to-sales ratio between 1987 and 1990. "These programs are management-intensive, rather than capital-intensive, succeeding by reorganizing the way in which work is done," Roubos stated in Dover's 1990 annual report.

The focus on productivity helped Dover weather one of the more difficult years in the corporation's history. Another economic recession reared in 1990, causing Dover's sales to fall 2 percent and its earnings per share to plummet 16 percent in 1991. Profits at Dover Elevator International alone plunged 40 percent: Building construction had dwindled to a virtual halt in the U. S., causing a sharp decline in new elevator manufacturing. Although Dover Elevator fared the worst, profits also were down at the other four subsidiaries. To ride out the

DOVER CORPORATION   TILT TOWARD GROWTH

crisis, many operating companies slashed employment levels, shuttered manufacturing plants, reduced fringe benefit programs, and froze salaries. Even Dover's corporate office did its share: The 1991 annual report was printed without color illustrations, paring its price tag by a third.

Roubos further responded to the exigencies of 1991 with an unprecedented divestment program. Several stand-alone and add-on acquisitions had failed to produce anticipated growth and were put on the block. The divestitures included Dover Japan (the marine seal product line of Waukesha Bearings), the Arbell and Quartztek operations of Dover Technologies, the Wolfe Frostop unit of Groen, Dover Technologies' Nurad operation, and Waukesha's PME division. Some operating companies were liquidated; others were merged into remaining concerns. "The recession made all too clear the weakness of a few of our product lines," Roubos explains.

For the first time in Dover's history, the proceeds of businesses sold exceeded the cost of businesses acquired—$13 million for six small elevator service companies, an electronics assembly business, and a product line for Tranter. On the bright side, the divestments along with Dover's relatively strong internal free-cash-flow generation increased the corporation's liquidity. Roubos invested $39 million of the cash in the corporation's common stock, which had held strong during the economic

BEARING UP

In the early 1990s, Waukesha Bearings shifted focus from manufacturing marine bearings to engineering bearings for the industrial turbomachinery market. Waukesha builds bearings to fit any application, including larger bearings such as the hydrodynamic bearing, left.

CULTURE: LEAN MACHINE

Few, if any, $5 billion corporations can boast Dover's remarkably lean corporate headquarters. The sparse Dover corporate office is housed in leased space on the thirty-fourth floor of 280 Park Avenue. This is in keeping with a tradition dating to the corporation's origin fifty years ago. George Ohrstrom had neither the experience nor interest in running a multi-industry conglomerate, preferring to expend his energies doing what he did best—buying companies. He turned over the management of Dover to former C. Lee Cook president Fred Durham, with the promise Durham could run the corporation from Cook's headquarters in Louisville, Kentucky. When Dover moved to new corporate offices in Washington, D.C., shortly after Ohrstrom's death, the staff consisted of Durham, his secretary, and a newly hired finance officer.

Durham believed the operations of Dover's constituent companies were best left to the capable individuals who had successfully managed them in the past; hence, there was no need to bolster his small staff with the usual array of vice presidents to centrally manage such activities as purchasing, advertising, or marketing. Over the years, as Dover itself grew in size, the corporate staff remained relatively static. In 1962, for instance, seven people were on the payroll. In 1965, Durham's successor, Tom Sutton, said Dover had "what is probably one of the smallest levels of any comparable company: four executives and ten supporting staff." Three years later, he no longer qualified his statement, stating unequivocally that Dover had "the smallest headquarters staff of any corporation of comparable size."

By the end of 1989, Dover's headquarters had "swelled" to twenty-one full-time employees. Keep in mind, though, that the corporation then numbered thirty-seven operating companies, a far cry from the four companies from which it had sprung. When Dover CEO Ron Hoffman's Tulsa Winch company joined Dover in 1996, he recalls his astonishment upon visiting the Manhattan headquarters and counting only thirty-six people at headquarters. "I think we have forty people here today—on a good day," Hoffman says. "I hope no one has the idea of fifty people here," he confides. "I sure don't."

DOVER CORPORATION   TILT TOWARD GROWTH

LEADERSHIP: THE RESTRUCTURER

Gary Roubos was born in Denver in 1936, the only child of working-class parents. His mother was a registered nurse, who reared him to excel academically. His father was a traveling salesman who spent most of the year on the road hawking automobile polish in eleven Southwestern states. The company eventually went under, compelling the family to move from one home to another as Roubos's father went from one job to the next. "The thing that always strikes me when I look back at my life is the immense distance I have traveled," he says.

Roubos, Dover's CEO from 1981 to 1994, rose to the highest echelon in corporate business through a combination of smarts and grit. As a teenager, he cut lawns, dug ditches, cleaned tanks at the Rocky Mountain Arsenal, and worked in the factory of a paper box company. When school resumed every September, he applied himself with equal vigor and diligence.

The hard work paid off: He received a full scholarship in 1954 to the University of Colorado. He majored in chemical engineering but took so many business courses that it took him five years to graduate. After a two-year stint as an officer in the United States Army's Corps of Engineers—Roubos had been in the

siege. Indeed, one of the few silver linings of 1991 was Dover's 15.9 percent return on equity, a percentage below its historical average but still a superior result for an industrial company in a recession year. By contrast, the average ROE for the Fortune 500 was 10.2 percent.

Since 1988, Dover had repurchased 10 percent of its own stock, an indication, according to a 1992 article in Fortune magazine, that the corporation "likes its prospects." The article in Fortune was one of the few times that Dover received such broad national publicity. Preferring humility to hubris, the corporation did not curry media attention, and its executive officers typically eschewed interviews other than to comment on Dover's financial results. Rather, it was left up to the operating companies to stake their own courses when it came to publicity, and many were covered fully by the business press.

The Fortune story was an exception to the rule. The writer introduced Dover to a public that, to a large extent, had not heard of it. "This manufacturer of mundane products like flow meters and gas pumps has 49 separate businesses operating in every state and more than two dozen foreign countries, [achieving] a return on shareholders' equity of fifteen percent to twenty percent, while typically holding debt to less than fifteen percent of total capital," the article stated. "Yet it operates with . . . no sales department, personnel, legal affairs or marketing.

Reserve Officer Training Corps in college—he applied to Harvard Businesss School and was accepted in 1961. His academic focus was manufacturing. "It was intellectual boot camp," Roubos says.

He graduated with honors in 1963 and subsequently received a number of job offers. He took one from Boise Cascade, working as a salesman before being promoted to general manager. He stayed in that position for three years, until he was transferred to the company's plant in St. Paul, Minnesota. "I became the assistant general manager, which I viewed as a step down," he recalls. "I stayed a year and then looked for another job."

Roubos found it at Dieterich Standard, a small company in New Buffalo, Michigan, that manufactured flow measurement instruments. Roubos was hired as the company's international sales manager, traveling the world as his father had once traveled the Southwest. By the time Dover Corporation came with an offer to buy the company in 1975, Roubos had built Dieterich's foreign sales to 40 percent of its revenue base. He also had become the company's president and part-owner, having accumulated a 10 percent stake.

When Tom Sutton cast his net for a CEO to replace himself in the late 1970s, he drew in a prized catch. Roubos served as Sutton's second in command for a few years, and, as CEO and later chairman, directed Dover's substantial restructuring in the mid-1980s.

HAIL TO THE CHIEF
Gary Roubos retained the Dover culture of encouraging autonomous management of operating companies. The red bandana presented to Gary Roubos by Heil President Larry Gray in 1993, below, commemorates the Dover CEO's visit to the Phoenix plant.

No fancy artwork on the walls of its unassuming Manhattan office, no corporate dining room, and no corporate jet idling out on the runway. About the only extravagance is [Roubos's] long, pointed mustache." A money manager quoted in the story said: "You'd never know it was a Fortune 500 company."

The magazine added that Dover "has remained true to its philosophy of buying good companies, setting ambitious targets for managers, motivating them with incentives, and then getting out of their way. And staying out." Dover's unique philosophy was now out in the open and soon became the subject of university business courses.

The forty-nine operating companies that comprised Dover in 1992 boasted a remarkable parallel: They all had been acquisitions at some point in Dover's history. But the recession of 1991, combined with intensified competition in the acquisitions arena, raised the distressing possibility of fewer acquisitions and, hence, slower growth in the years ahead. In 1993, Dover's executive officers initiated discussions and analysis of a new growth strategy, dubbed the "Tilt Toward Growth" by CFO John McNiff, to reconnect the corporation's growth priorities to the realities of the changing business climate.

DOVER CORPORATION TILT TOWARD GROWTH

CHANGE SESSION

Competition heated up in the mid-1990s for the kinds of companies that Dover traditionally courted. Dover's board of directors, here at a 1993 board meeting in the Mississippi State Capitol Building, challenged operating company presidents to pursue add-on acquisitions.

The "Tilt," as it would be called within Dover, realigned executives' incentive compensations with their companies' economic value creation: The greater a company's value creation, the higher an executive's incentive reward.

The new line of attack represents a key milestone in the corporation's history. The new plan challenged operating company presidents to pursue a more aggressive growth strategy that encouraged add-on acquisitions,

A more important factor was a shift in the *kind* of acquisitions that Dover needed to make. The increasing globalization of manufacturing had changed the business landscape, requiring manufacturers like those within Dover to think and act globally. With 96 percent of the world's consumers living outside the United States and representing a vast, largely untapped market, U.S. manufacturers had to tackle the difficult issue of whether to manufacture at home and export or to produce

"FOR YEARS, THE WHOLE CONCEPT WAS 'NO SYNERGY' WHEN IT CAME TO ACQUISITIONS. WE NEEDED TO REVISE OUR THINKING. AND WE DID THAT WITH THE TILT."

— Tom Reece, Dover Corporation CEO (1994–2004)

and then rewarded them for their financial successes. In effect, the burden was placed on the presidents to grow their companies by investing Dover capital in acquiring other companies. Roubos is credited with early development of the strategy, but the new direction would not bear fruit until the term of Tom Reece, Roubos's successor as Dover's CEO.

The impetus for the new direction was clear: The subsidiaries and operating companies were not growing as needed to sustain Dover's historical shareholder returns. Competition to acquire the kind of companies Dover had historically favored had increased markedly; from 1989 through 1992, the corporation had acquired only nine companies.

abroad. The answer for each company depended upon an analysis of many factors, including the availability of labor, capital, and raw materials; the proximity to markets; transportation costs; shipping costs and feasibility; and prevailing political, regulatory, legal, and tax environments. To continue its historical growth pattern, Dover needed to compete outside the United States; and, to compete and win in the global marketplace, Dover operating companies needed to acquire foreign companies with complementary products or to branch into those markets de novo.

The challenge confronting Roubos and Reece was how to motivate Dover companies to act more globally in terms of their add-on acquisitions—expanding

IN THE OPEN

Until *Fortune* magazine profiled Dover in a 1992 article, few outside its markets had heard of the corporation. The article commented on the Dover Philosophy—the singular tenets of organization and management that distinguished Dover from other conglomerates.

DOVER CORPORATION TILT TOWARD GROWTH

INNOVATION: HEIL'S DURAPACK HALF/PACK

Heil Environmental Industries enjoys a long reputation as an innovator. It produced the world's first electrically welded tank, the first tin-lined milk truck, the first twin-arm hydraulic hoists for truck bodies, the first mobile crop dehydrators, and the first fully hydraulic steering mechanism. When Heil entered the refuse collection vehicle body market, the innovations continued. The company is the manufacturer of the DuraPack Half/Pack garbage truck loader, the standard to which all other front loaders are compared. The Half/Pack also is legendary for its productivity, boasting clamp-on arms rated for more than 8,000 pounds of lift and a body that is capable of packing more than 1,000 pounds per cubic yard of refuse. From its John Deere cylinders to the patented clamp-on arms to the reliable controls and on-board diagnostics, Half/Pack is a class of its own.

geographic boundaries, technology platforms, product lines, distribution arrangements, and customer service capabilities. "The concept in Dover for many years was one of 'sticking to your knitting,' running your own business and thinking in terms of product development and market expansion; but, as the world became more global, our companies had to think in those terms, as well," explains Reece, who became Roubos's executive vice president and chief operating officer in 1993 and who was in on the ground floor of planning and instituting the "Tilt."

"We didn't really have people looking at buying smaller companies overseas or domestically with a product line that complemented their products or geographic distribution that they didn't have," he adds. "Indeed, we bought a lot of our own stock in the late eighties because we had all this cash and no well-conceived add-on acquisition strategy. So Gary and I began thinking strongly about a more formal, strategic add-on acquisition program, spending a lot of time clarifying what a good add-on acquisition would look like. For years, the whole concept was 'no synergy' when it came to acquisitions. We needed to revise our thinking. And we did that with the Tilt."

Add-on acquisitions were not a new concept, of course. But Dover had not formalized a policy and process for undertaking that activity. "We always did add-on acquisitions, particularly at the elevator company, where a company would be acquired for its product line or to consolidate distribution, or for some other specific tactical purpose," says Robert Tyre, who replaced Ed Kata as Dover's acquisitions specialist in 1994. "But these kinds of acquisitions weren't necessarily strategic in nature, and they had always taken a back seat to stand-alone acquisitions—the historical precedent of the company. Everyone focused on stand-alone acquisitions because that is what Ohrstrom, Durham, and Sutton had

TOP OF THE HEAP

In 1945, Heil Environmental Industries produced the first refuse body that could compress waste loads to achieve higher capacity. The 1955 Colecto-Pak used the combination of a sweeping blade and rear-loading hopper to clear and compact garbage.

HOT PROPERTY

Acquired in 1978, Tranter is a leading manufacturer of heat transfer and cooling equipment. Tranter began life in the 1930s as a maker of eutectic plates for milk trucks, and is now known for its comprehensive range of plate heat exchangers, below, used in a variety of applications.

done, buying niche companies with leading market share and solid managements that would stick around; and, meanwhile, there would be no integration and no synergy, just autonomous operations. That's what always worked and it was undeniably successful. Add-on acquisitions, on the other hand, entered the realm of synergistic acquisitions, which, historically, were shunned."

The challenges and opportunities posed by competition and globalization required a new course, one that would direct add-on acquisitions for strategic, long-term purposes, such as entering a new geographic market or acquiring an important new technology. Company presidents were given virtually free rein to negotiate and make acquisitions they deemed essential to growth, with analytical input from Dover's corporate office and the subsidiaries in which their companies resided. It was the president's call whether to integrate an acquired concern or to operate it separately or at arm's length. "Basically, we decided that 'synergy' was good so long as it was properly defined and quantified as strategic," says Tyre.

The "Tilt Toward Growth" campaign did not kick into gear, but rather achieved traction slowly. From 1994 forward, Dover's operating companies would grow and strengthen via an unprecedented number of add-on acquisitions. "It wasn't like the Oklahoma Land Rush where this gun went off and everyone was out grabbing companies and pounding stakes into the ground," Tyre says. "The program evolved. The first few add-on acquisitions were what we expected—companies buying their counterparts in Europe, such as Tranter acquiring Sweden's HTT/Swep and Tipper Tie acquiring Germany's Technopak. And, then, after Tom Reece became CEO in May 1994, the pace really picked up."

Dover executed ten acquisitions at a cost of $185 million in 1994, representing the corporation's third largest year for acquisition investment. Unlike prior years, the majority of that investment, roughly 65 percent, was spent on acquisitions that were additive to existing Dover operating companies. For example, Blackmer, DE-STA-CO, and Phoenix Refrigeration Systems, which Dover had bought in 1993, all made add-on acquisitions in 1994 in deals negotiated by their respective presidents.

The example of Phoenix Refrigeration offers an illustration of a successful add-on acquisition strategy at work. The company, which makes refrigerated systems for supermarket display cases, acquired Hill Refrigeration, Inc., a maker of display cases, enabling the combined Hill PHOENIX to manufacture complete units and, thereby, compete more effectively in the marketplace. "This is something an operating company can think about now when thinking about growing their business," Reece asserts. "It's another tool in the toolbox."

In 1995, Dover shareholders approved by proxy a new executive compensation package that would spur add-on acquisitions through the remainder of the decade. The new compensation plan maintained the competitive level of annual cash compensation but significantly expanded the long-term gain opportunities for operating managers, particularly company presidents, who achieved superior growth that created stockholder value. In effect, the multiplier for the axis measuring average annual percentage growth in earnings over three years was

APPETIZING ACQUISITION

Dover acquired Phoenix Refrigeration in 1993 and Hill Refrigeration in 1994, combining the two companies into Hill PHOENIX. Today Hill PHOENIX is a leading maker of refrigerated display cases, like this high-end deli case.

DOVER CORPORATION TILT TOWARD GROWTH

AUTONOMY: UPWARD CLIMB

The story of Hill PHOENIX is one of bold vision, strong leadership, and the will to venture beyond borders. It begins with Phoenix Refrigeration Systems, which Dover acquired in 1993. Like other opportunistic acquisitions, Phoenix Refrigeration had what it took to be a Dover operating company. It was a market leader in the manufacture of commercial refrigeration systems for cooling supermarket display cases, had recorded excellent growth through the years, and boasted very strong, entrepreneurial management.

"Grant Brown had founded the company just outside Atlanta and was a very well-respected fellow in the refrigeration industry," says Jerry Yochum, who, as CEO of Dover Diversified, handled the negotiations to buy Phoenix Refrigeration. "Grant liked the Dover way of doing things, and I liked the company's earnings and profitability prospects, plus the fact that the numbers on the deal were right," he adds. "Everything fit."

Like other Dover operating company presidents, Brown ran Phoenix Refrigeration as if he still owned the business. The ink was barely dry on the deal when Brown approached Yochum about an add-on acquisition he had in mind, Hill Refrigeration, Inc., which manufactured refrigerated display cases. "Grant had argued that supermarket chains were beginning to bundle their purchases and wanted to buy both the refrigeration and the cases from the same company," Yochum comments. "It was a good idea except for the fact that Hill was a pretty troubled company, floundering and on the market as distressed merchandise. I told Grant that Dover did not acquire companies in a turn-around situation. That just wasn't our thing. We buy good companies at a fair price, I explained. So I turned him down."

But Brown was persistent, convincing Yochum to take a deeper look at Hill, which had a good reputation. "The company was doing about $100 million a year in volume but was not making any money," Yochum recalls. "Grant had a vision for combining the two companies, and he prevailed upon me that this was the right thing to do. Ultimately, he persuaded me he was right. We bought Hill in 1994 from Eagle Industries for less than asset value and immediately merged the two companies." The combined entity, renamed Hill PHOENIX, was relocated to a new state-of-the-art manufacturing facility in Richmond, Virginia.

Sadly, Brown died in a light-plane crash shortly after the merger. "Here we had made our first acquisition of a turn-around company and had just lost the visionary," sighs Tom Reece, Dover CEO at the time. "It was a major struggle. Then we found this terrific fellow who had cut his teeth at General Electric named Ralph Coppola. He came through, turning Hill PHOENIX into one of our better companies over the years."

Hill PHOENIX today is the industry's most innovative supermarket refrigeration and display case manufacturer, meeting customers' needs with customized solutions rather than standard offerings.

HILLTOP GRAZING
Hill Refrigeration, today's Hill PHOENIX, was founded by C. V. Hill, a New Jersey grocer who designed and built a novel refrigerated case for use at his shop. Word of the remarkable cases spread, compelling Hill in 1889 to build a factory to make them. Above: A Hill case circa 1920.

increased. "We needed to energize our growth engine, and the old matrix rewarded individuals even when growth was stagnant," Reece explains. "You could get an extraordinary incentive reward with up to minus 5 percent real-earnings decline. Heck, that's no way to spur growth. So we tilted the old matrix to emphasize earnings growth over return on investment."

Tyre comments, "The message before the change was, 'Send Dover your cash, and we'll make the acquisitions'; the message after was, 'Make add-on acquisitions if the earnings growth is sufficient to justify the inevitable reduction in return on investment, since investment will increase by virtue of the price paid for the add-on acquisition.' This was a strong signal that really kicked off the add-on program."

Once the compensation plan was in effect, the "Tilt" inclined even further. Dover set a record for acquisition activity in 1995, investing $323 million in two stand-alone and seven add-on acquisitions. The largest add-on acquisition was AT&T Frequency Control Products, acquired by Vectron Labs, a Dover stand-alone acquisition in 1992. The combined company, renamed Vectron Technologies, gave Dover global leadership in the precision crystal oscillator market. Vectron also boasted enviable intellectual capital, including several executives from AT&T who would guide and execute numerous add-on acquisitions in succeeding years.

Among these was the 2004 acquisition of Corning's Frequency Control business. This acquisition brought strategic and complementary products and roughly doubled Vectron's sales and earnings.

Overall, Dover's acquisition activity during the three years of 1993 to 1995 totaled $830 million, more than the corporation had invested on acquisitions in the preceding ten years. Of that total, more than $240 million represented strategic add-on acquisitions.

HIGH FREQUENCY

In the 1990s, Dover acquired AT&T Frequency Control Products and Vectron Laboratories, which combined to form Vectron International, a world leader in frequency generation and control products. Today, Vectron products include customized crystal oscillators inside the Mars Rover spacecraft and the oscillators shown left.

INNOVATION: HILL PHOENIX'S COOLGENIX TECHNOLOGY

Hill PHOENIX developed the retail supermarket industry's first refrigerated top display case, which allowed customers to view the merchandise inside; the first all-metal case; and the first freezer case, which helped establish the retail frozen food business in grocery stores. More recently, Hill PHOENIX introduced its Coolgenix proprietary cooling technology, which reduces operating costs, extends shelf life, and enhances product displays at supermarkets. Coolgenix uses a secondary coolant technology to refrigerate products in their cases without any moving air. This is achieved by using a low-profile top gravity coil in conjunction with a roll-bonded, refrigerated bottom pan that cools through conduction. Retailers have embraced Coolgenix as a way to provide very dramatic display cases for meats and seafood, while at the same time extending product shelf life and reducing costs.

DOVER CORPORATION TILT TOWARD GROWTH

DOVER GENERATIONS

Tom Reece's unimpeachable character and impressive performance as president of three operating companies assured his predecessors that they were placing Dover in capable hands. Above: Reece—then a young operating company president—and Durham (right) wear festive party hats at Durham's last board meeting.

Tom Reece was the logical candidate to succeed Roubos. He not only had presided over three Dover operating companies—Ronningen-Petter, DE-STA-CO, and Norris—he had served as the CEO of Dover Resources, giving him broad, valuable experience. He was succeeded as CEO of Dover Resources by Rudy Herrmann, who had come to Dover via the acquisition of Texas Hydraulics and, after continuing as president of that company, had become president of Rotary Lift.

Reece had impressed Durham, Sutton, and Roubos with his candor and rock-solid American values. He was the third of six children born and reared on an eighty-acre farm in southwestern Michigan. His father supplemented his income from farming at the local paper mill, where he was a superintendent. Reece's mother was a schoolteacher, and Reece and his siblings gravitated toward that profession. After graduating from Western Michigan University in 1964, where he majored in biology, Reece took a position teaching biology and general sciences at the high school from which he had graduated. During summer months, he made extra money by soldering filters at Ronningen-Petter, where his older brother, Jack, also worked.

At the behest of Bill Petter, son-in-law of the founder and chairman of Ronningen-Petter, Reece left the world of teaching for the world of business. "Bill asked me in 1965 if I wanted to work in sales; he and the other sales guys at the company were always out in the field, and they needed a 'Mr. Inside,' someone who could put together brochures, answer calls from customers,

CULTURE: BEDROCK VALUES

"The CEO of Dover should have the following qualities: First, integrity." With those words, Dover CEO Fred Durham established a code of ethical leadership at Dover, its subsidiaries, and operating companies.

Durham had spent his early professional years working with Charles Lee Cook, the famed wheelchair-bound inventor, business leader, linguist, writer, and art historian of the early twentieth century, who remained optimistic at times of extraordinary duress, and never complained of his hardship. Cook believed, as he wrote, that success "simply means that we have got to give more than we receive." Durham often said Cook had taught him the "meaning of absolute integrity" in matters small and large. "He had more influence on my life, I suppose, than anybody, including my mother and father," Durham remarked.

The poet Ralph Waldo Emerson wrote, "An institution is the shadow of one man." In Dover's case, Durham is that man, establishing a credo of fairness, honesty, and candor that continues to guide Dover management as Charles Cook had guided him. Tom Sutton, Dover's second CEO, said of Durham: "Integrity was his whole being."

"It all began with Fred Durham," says Dover CEO Tom Reece. "His bedrock values were the foundation. Integrity was so important to him that he would pass on buying a terrific company offering great value if he did not believe the management of the company was honest. They could be iron-fisted or laissez-faire managers, but there had to be no question about their fundamental, underlying principles. If there was, the deal was dead in the water."

Sutton once commented that Dover presidents must possess the following traits: loyalty to employees, responsibility to customers, and a "moral obligation" to the corporation to do what is right—"to do the right things, as well as to do things right." The key to Dover's success, he said, is the quality of leadership at the operating companies. "We're a company that believes in autonomous management," Sutton explained. "I had to trust the presidents would make the right decisions. So, we made sure we had the right guys in the job."

Unimpeachable character assured Sutton that the presidents of the operating companies would, indeed, do the right things. Although their styles of leadership might differ, their veracity was critical. Sutton's successor as CEO, Gary Roubos, recalls meeting several Dover operating company presidents as part of his due diligence in selling his company, Dieterich Standard, to Dover in 1975. "They were very different people from a personality perspective, but they shared certain distinct values—honesty and integrity above all," Roubos comments.

Among those he met was Reece, who had cut his teeth at Ronningen-Petter, which Dover acquired in 1968. As a young Dover company president, the former high school science teacher recalls saving a year's compensation, "just in case I was ever asked to do something illegal or dishonest," he says. "It was my walk-away money." He never had to tap the funds and learned the beauty of compounding at an early age.

What does integrity mean to Tom Reece? "I remember we were looking at a potential acquisition of this company once, a company with great financials, but we passed on buying it," he says. "I'm not going to buy a company from somebody I couldn't take home and proudly introduce to my wife. A man's character—his reputation—is everything."

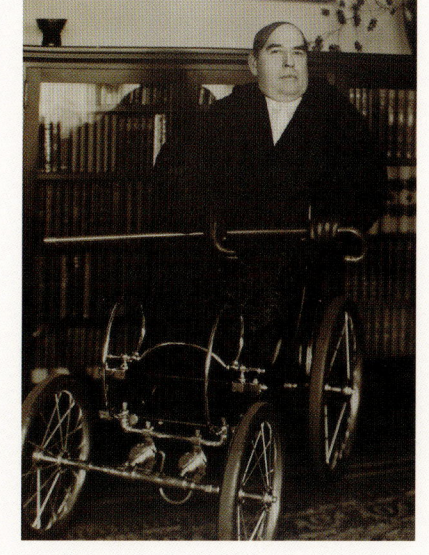

PROFILE IN COURAGE

An inventor, scholar, painter, linguist, businessman, and lawyer, Charles Lee Cook, founder of one of Dover's pillar companies, would not let infirmity deter his insatiable curiosity and dedication to self-improvement.

DOVER CORPORATION TILT TOWARD GROWTH

and send out mailings," Reece recalls. "I was pleased Bill came to me, and liked the fact that I would make 50 percent more money than I could make in a classroom. So I took the offer." He was twenty-two years old.

Reece rose quickly through the ranks, from inside sales to a post as advertising manager, learning everything he could about the filter business. When Dover purchased Ronningen-Petter in 1968 and named Bill Petter the president, Reece became head of sales and marketing. Two years later, Tony Ormsby asked Petter to succeed the president of Blackmer Pump, and, when Petter accepted, Ormsby inquired who could best succeed Petter at Ronningen-Petter. Without any hesitation, Petter offered up Reece. "Tom was very intelligent, capable, good to people, and completely straight up," Petter says. "It wasn't a difficult decision. You work with a guy and his family, and you get to know their integrity." Reece was twenty-eight years old, the youngest Dover operating company president in its history.

Although he never attended business school, Reece says he "picked things up at Kalamazoo College and Western Michigan—mostly all seminar stuff." He later tapped his native academic skills and became a stalwart student of business, devouring articles on diverse subjects, from Japanese manufacturing techniques to emerging enterprise technologies to macroeconomic social trends. He also credits Petter with furthering his development—"real mentoring," he says.

FOUR ACES

For a majority of Dover's first fifty years, there remained a tie between Dover's first CEO and its most recent. Photographed in 1995 with Fred Durham (seated) are (left to right) Tom Reece, Gary Roubos, and Tom Sutton.

Each time he headed a Dover company, Reece not only became an expert on its business and industry, he restructured it into a more modern organization. As Dover CEO, he would be both articulate and ardent about business; in his desk drawer he keeps a toggle clamp from his days of running DE-STA-CO and delights in describing its features to visitors.

Reece also had no intention of scuttling Dover's business model. "I'm not coming in as an agent of change, but as an agent of perpetuation," he told *Business Week* magazine in January 1995, eight months after becoming CEO. Reece would maintain Dover's lean staff and barebones head office—the magazine described it as looking "like a dentist's office"—and would respect the boundaries of autonomous operations at Dover's fifty-four companies. As a former operating company president, Reece firmly believed in the value of independent leadership. "I had been the president of Ronningen-Petter for about six months, and remember thinking I wasn't particularly happy with what I was doing," he confides. "I woke up one day and said to myself, 'Tom, you're not running the business the way you would run it, but the way Bill Petter ran it.' He was my mentor and I admired and liked him, of course, but in the final analysis we were very different people, with different styles of leadership and management. I thought, 'I can't be Bill anymore; I have to be myself—own this business and run it the way I see fit.' I had to do it my way. It's a message I give to operating company presidents to this day." Taking his cue from his predecessors, Reece's first task, as he saw it, was to "get out and visit the companies."

The Reece era would mark a significant departure from the tenure of Roubos, who remained Dover's chairman. Roubos is credited with restructuring Dover and launching the "Tilt Toward Growth," but it is Reece who would do much of the "tilting," angling Dover to become what *Business Week* called "a perpetual acquisition machine, a case study of the art of the deal."

Assisting him in the effort was a very capable team including the subsidiaries' CEOs and CFOs; Bob Tyre, Dover's vice president of corporate development and all-around acquisitions specialist; John McNiff, Dover's vice president of finance and chief financial officer; and Rob Kuhbach, Dover's vice president and general counsel and later chief financial officer.

Tyre grew up in Garden City, New York, and graduated from Williams College in 1967, earned his master's of business administration at New York University's School of Business, and later his law degree from Fordham University Law School. In the 1970s, Tyre worked for National Cash Register in Dayton, Ohio, and U.S. Industries, joining the latter's corporate development department and gaining invaluable experience in buying and selling companies. At night, he attended law school "to be on equal footing with the lawyers I had to deal with in this line of work," he says. After receiving his law degree in 1982, he accepted a position in the acquisition services unit of consulting firm Booz Allen, ascending to become a partner and head of the firm's U.S. acquisitions business.

McNiff, credited with coining the "Tilt Toward Growth" phrase, joined Dover in 1983. After earning a bachelor's degree in economics and mathematics from Princeton University and an MBA from Stanford

THE DOVER WAY

Business Week magazine's January 1995 feature story, titled "Who Says the Conglomerate is Dead," praised Dover's culture, lauding its encouragement of risk-taking and entrepreneurship by the corporation's fifty-four operating company presidents.

DOVER CORPORATION   TILT TOWARD GROWTH

AT THE CENTER

Bob Tyre, above, came to Dover as its vice president of corporate development and all-around acquisition specialist. Right: Rob Kuhbach (left) serves as Dover's vice president of finance and chief financial officer while Joseph Schmidt, who succeeded Kuhbach, is vice president, general counsel, and secretary.

University, McNiff had spent virtually his entire career at The Allen Group, Inc., a manufacturer of automotive products. McNiff had worked his way up to the number two position at Allen, as executive vice president of finance, administration, and international, in which capacity he oversaw a staff of seventy employees. Upon his hiring, former Dover CEO Gary Roubos quipped that McNiff "will have to get used to operating with a much smaller staff."

Kuhbach had a broad corporate background. He joined Dover in February 1993 as Dover's first general counsel, replacing longtime corporate counsel Cloyd Laporte, Jr., who retired. Kuhbach had earned a bachelor of arts degree in economics from Yale University and a law degree from University of Michigan Law School. After almost eight years of corporate, securities law, and litigation experience at a major New York law firm, Kuhbach went to work "inside" at two diversified industrial companies. He spent nine years at General Host Corporation, becoming general counsel and handling major acquisitions, divestitures, and financing. He then moved to Sudbury, Inc., in 1989, eventually becoming executive vice president, general counsel, and corporate secretary. Sudbury's primary operations included automotive parts production, metal fabrication, and lubricants. The company, previously a member of the Fortune 500, eventually had to be reorganized under Chapter 11 bankruptcy, which Kuhbach successfully completed in eight months, leading to Sudbury's full recovery by the end of 1992.

Ironically, Tyre had first come to Dover's attention in 1983 to succeed Cam Caswell, but the job instead went to Ed Kata. "It was a good thing I wasn't hired then because my time at Booz Allen was the best education anyone could have asked for," Tyre maintains. "I consulted to hundreds of corporations on their merger, acquisition, and divestiture plans, from evaluation to negotiation to post-sale integration." When the same executive search firm that had introduced him to Dover in 1983 mentioned the corporation again was looking for an acquisitions specialist, Tyre asked the executive recruiter, David Chambers, to ferret out his introductory letter from eleven years earlier. "He found it, and I added an addendum, tacking on the things I did since, which were considerable," he says. "It was a damn good letter in the first place."

Tyre had left Booz Allen to establish his own boutique mergers and acquisitions consulting business when Chambers called. "I figured if I didn't get the job, I might generate some business for my firm," he says. "Frankly, I really wasn't all that interested in the position. But then I met Tom and we hit it off. He was people-oriented and instinctive, and I thought, 'This is a guy I can work with.' I warmed to him right away. And I believed in his vision." As a team, Reece and Tyre would refine the intellectual framework for the "Tilt Toward Growth" campaign and guide its vigorous maturation over the years.

AUTONOMY: THE ORIGINS OF HEIL

Two Dover Corporation companies—Heil Environmental Industries, Ltd., and Heil Trailer International—were spawned from a company founded nearly a century ago by Julius Heil, whose hard-won success in business culminated in his election as the governor of the state of Wisconsin in 1938.

Born on his family's small farm in rural Wisconsin, Julius quit school at the age of twelve to assist his father on the farm and earn additional money as a stock boy at a local general store. Two years later, he left home for the big city of Milwaukee, working a variety of jobs, from drill press operator in a machine shop to streetcar conductor in the city's emerging street railway system. He then caught the attention of Herman Falk, the owner of a local wagon shop, who had a radical idea—welding together streetcar rails instead of securing them with wire, as was the customary practice. Falk converted some traditional welding equipment into a machine that could generate enough heat to fuse rails together, and he hired Julius to supervise one of his welding crews.

Julius loved the work. Supervising his welding crew in Washington, D.C., once, he had the opportunity to explain the novel process to President William McKinley, who had stopped his carriage to observe Julius's crew in action. Julius later had the occasion to supervise a welding crew for another company that had been contracted in the late 1890s to develop Argentina's burgeoning rail system. In 1901, Julius figured he had developed enough expertise to start his own welding company, and he incorporated the Heil Rail Joint Welding Company. With $25,000 in venture capital, he leased a small factory, hired a few employees, and, to conserve expenses, paid himself a paltry salary of two dollars a month. But the company lost money in its first year and barely scraped by. In 1906, it was liquidated to pay off debts.

Undeterred, Julius launched The Heil Company to focus on a welding market beyond rails, welding together smokestacks and milk tanks, among other manufactured products. Business started slowly, but by 1907 the company recorded $5,501.16 in earnings, a respectable amount. Julius invested the money in a new 9,600–square foot plant in Milwaukee and branched into other markets, including the making of steel truck bodies.

In 1919, Heil acquired Hydro Hoist Company, which manufactured dump body hoists. In 1937, Heil entered the refuse collection equipment market to supply New York City with garbage truck bodies featuring Heil's innovative rear-loading hoppers. The new product line blossomed quickly; by the 1940s, motorized Heil refuse collection bodies collected solid waste in hundreds of American cities, making Heil the market leader, a position the company has retained to the present.

Julius Heil capitalized on his reputation in business circles by entering the political arena. In 1938, he was elected to Wisconsin's highest office, serving one term as governor. His son and grandson led the company through 1993, when it was sold to Dover Corporation. Two years later, Dover split Heil in two, a decision predicated on the two major markets the company plied—the manufacturing of waste- and recycling-collection bodies and the manufacturing of petroleum and dry-bulk tank trailers. Both companies today are guided by something the founder said almost a century ago: "Build it right and then back it with integrity."

HAIL HEIL

Julius Heil's life is the classic American success story. Although Heil, above, quit school at the age of twelve to help run the family farm, he later founded and presided over a successful company.

DOVER CORPORATION TILT TOWARD GROWTH

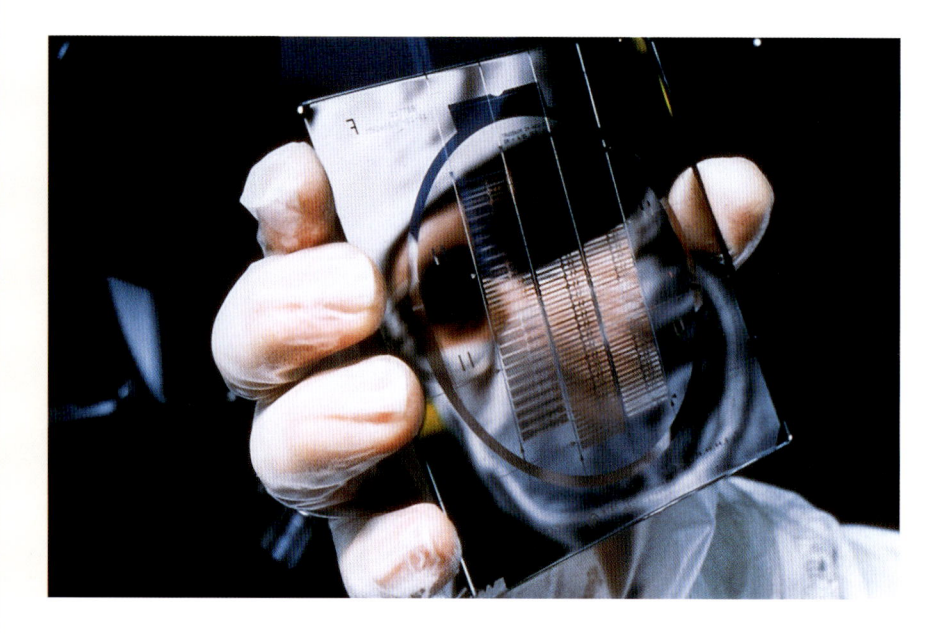

INDELIBLE LEGACY

In the 1990s, Vectron Labs—today Vectron International—contributed to Dover Technologies' success. With the acquisition of Vectron in 1992, Dover became an important player in the precision crystal oscillator market. Above: Wafer metallization is an initial step in oscillator construction.

Although add-on acquisitions accounted for much of the "Tilt" in the mid-1990s, the corporation, through the subsidiaries, also made several large stand-alone acquisitions, such as Belvac, Vectron, and Phoenix. In 1993, Dover also acquired Heil Company, a century-old maker of refuse collection vehicle bodies and tankers. At the time of its acquisition, Heil was the largest company in Dover Industries and the third largest in Dover Corporation. Shortly thereafter, Heil was reorganized into two companies: Heil Environmental, which focuses on the refuse and recycling collection vehicle market; and Heil Trailer International, which targets the liquid and dry-bulk trailer and container markets. Both companies are part of Dover Industries.

Eager to fund more acquisitions, Reece launched the first public offering of long-term debt securities in Dover's history in 1995, issuing $250 million in ten-year notes, which were rated A-plus by Standard & Poor's. Dover acquired two stand-alone companies that year, each serving different segments of the commercial/industrial printing business: Mark Andy, Inc., whose flexographic presses are used primarily to print self-adhesive labels and tags that identify consumer goods products; and Imaje, S.A., a French company considered one of the market leaders in the manufacture of continuous ink-jet printing equipment, which is used to mark "sell by" dates and other information on beverage and food packages. Mark Andy joined Dover Diversified; Imaje joined Dover Technologies.

Imaje constituted Dover's first large acquisition of a non-U.S. manufacturing concern and also was the corporation's largest acquisition at that time, purchased at auction for approximately $200 million. The company was a leader in its market and was under the care of capable management but had encountered market troubles during the early 1990s recession. A devaluation of the French franc and an ill-timed product release that resulted in a costly recall had undermined Imaje, necessitating a recapitalization by its French banks. The banks, led by Credit Lyonnais, which had the controlling ownership, decided to sell the company in 1995 as it recovered from its troubles of the early 1990s.

Tyre, who found the acquisition candidate by calling on Credit Lyonnais's New York office, was convinced Imaje was a world-class organization deserving Dover's scrutiny, and he brought the company to the attention of Pomeroy, who was looking for a business that would counter the cyclicality of the electronics companies within Dover Technologies. "Imaje was an exceptional financial deal that put Dover solidly in Europe," Reece says. "It also guided our decision to open an office in

London to chart a more formal international acquisition strategy." Buying Imaje further sent a clear message to the subsidiaries about Dover's projected course, "encouraging people to think more geographically and expansively in their stand-alone acquisitions," Reece asserts.

Dover Technologies was the standout Dover subsidiary in the latter half of the 1990s. The unit led all others in sales each year from 1995 through 1999; in the first half of 2000, its sales were 60 percent more than those reported by the next biggest subsidiary, Dover Industries, and its profits were twice as large. The lion's share of Dover Technologies' gains was produced by Universal Instruments, which grew spectacularly during the decade of the 1990s to become Dover's biggest contributor to growth, much as the earnings of W. C. Norris had fueled the corporation in the 1970s.

Universal dominated the through-hole component-insertion equipment market but had been challenged in the late 1980s and early 1990s by a new technology—surface-mount equipment. With Dover capital, Universal had invested substantially in research and development and soon entered that market, broadening its product lineup to include equipment for component centering and pinpoint part placement. The company then had embarked on an ambitious program to further increase its standing in the market by the introduction of its first surface-mount GSM-1 machine in 1993.

HIGH TECHNOLOGY

Dover Technologies' market success during the latter half of the 1990s and into 2000 was substantial. Every high-tech part that the subsidiary's operating companies manufactured was in demand, including frequency translators, used in microwave transmission towers like the one here.

DOVER CORPORATION   TILT TOWARD GROWTH

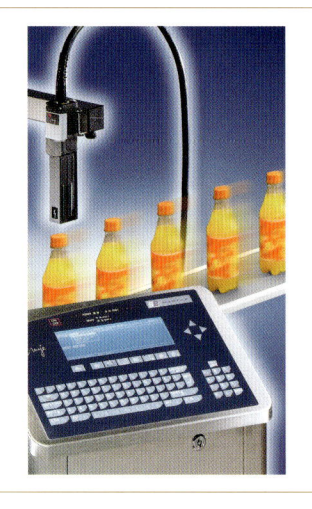

INNOVATION: IMAJE'S SERIES-8 PRINTER

From its breakthrough printing technology in the early 1980s to its inspired product identification solutions today, Imaje Group has earned its distinction as an international leader in the design and manufacture of industrial and commercial marking equipment and consumable supplies. Founded in Bourg-les-Valence, France, in 1982, Imaje raised the bar with its Series-1 printer, which could be used to mark even the delicate curved shell of an egg. Improved versions of the printer have been unveiled over the years, leading to the latest iteration, the versatile Series-8 printer, which can mark on all types of products and on all surfaces, under the most difficult, dusty, damp, or hot conditions with a wide range of inks—food grade, high contrast, or even invisible. The Series-8 printer is considered the cost-effective solution to the coding and marking needs of all types of industries today, including pharmaceuticals, food, beverage, aerospace, and heavy engineering.

The GSM line positioned Universal to make major market inroads through the 1990s, transforming the company into a major-league player in the surface-mount portion of the electronic circuit board assembly equipment business, a $4 billion market by the end of the decade. Meanwhile, Universal continued to dominate the through-hole segment of the market. As circuit boards found diverse applications in the electronics, telecommunications, computer, and automotive industries and were used in everything from cell phones and laptop computers to CD and DVD players, Universal reaped the financial rewards. Not all years were stellar for the company, given the cyclical volatility of the technology sector, but most years produced substantial gains in bookings and sales. In 1995, for instance, Universal set a profit record by a wide margin on record sales of more than $500 million.

The profits garnered by Universal were cited as a factor in helping Dover record a cumulative three-year earnings gain of 110 percent through 1995, the highest in the company's history at the time. In nine of the last ten ten-year periods, an investment in Dover, on an after-tax basis, had outperformed the Standard & Poor's 500, positioning Dover in the upper echelon of corporate performers. Four events underpinned the corporation's solid success: the rebound of Universal Instruments; Dover's growing international presence; the record acquisition activity; and a reorganized elevator operation. Dover Elevator International was reconfigured into a unitary business, with a factory operation and three field organizations reporting to a single president as opposed to the collection of loosely affiliated businesses that historically had characterized the company. The reorganization boosted Dover Elevator's profits by 179 percent in 1996.

Amid the larger success stories were smaller ones such as that of OPW Fueling Components. OPW transformed its factory from traditional assembly line manufacturing processes to cellular manufacturing in which workstations, or "cells," are arranged in such a way that the product can be processed progressively from one workstation to another without having to wait for a batch to be completed and without additional handling between operations. As part of the new system, OPW invested in new machining tools and then trained employees to operate more than one machine. At the end of 1996, the company listed only two job classifications, compared to twenty previously. Those changes combined to shorten production times substantially, enabling OPW to build parts to order for the first time in its history.

Similar gains by other operating companies added up to produce big gains for Dover. "Continuous improvement of products, processes, and skills is the most important factor underlying Dover's growth expectations for future years," Reece stated in Dover's 1996 annual report.

With Reece at the wheel, Dover continued its "Tilt Toward Growth," making two more stand-alone acquisitions in 1996. Everett Charles Technologies (ECT) became the second largest acquisition in Dover's history at the time. The company had established three separate market-leading niches in the electronic test market with such products as equipment to test circuitry on printed circuit boards before the boards are populated with components. Most important from Dover's perspective, ECT was a "platform company," a company ripe for further growth via add-on acquisitions. "A platform acquisition subscribed to the traditional Dover criteria

THE OLD GUARD

Older Dover operating companies like OPW remained at the top of their industries in the 1990s. Right: An employee assembles OPW nozzles using state-of-the-art ergonomic tooling.

INNOVATION: ECT'S ELIMINATOR TESTER

Since 1965, Everett Charles Technologies has played the leading role in the development of advanced technology in the bare and loaded circuit boards and semiconductor electrical test product market. Its newest disruptive technology is the Eliminator tester, which does away with costly test fixtures for testing bare printed circuit boards while reducing the time spent waiting for fixture fabrication. The machine can test multi-image panels with 50,000 test points, as well as dense ball-grid array patterns and fine pitch pads, at 10 ohms continuity in two minutes—the fastest time in the industry. Eliminator also effectively eliminates the density, pitch, and pad size limitations of pinned fixtures. Long the market leader in electrical test solutions, ECT boasts extensive R&D capabilities and enjoys an enviable core competency in its ability to make an electrical contact with the device or unit under test.

---

for an operating company, while being in a market that offered significant growth through add-on acquisitions," Reece explains.

For a year, Pomeroy had courted ECT's president and principal shareholder, Dave Van Loan, who was reluctant to sell the company. Van Loan had engineered several small acquisitions in building ECT, but, as the company became more successful, he was disinclined to make additional acquisitions. "Dave was playing with real dollars that were largely his own now, and he became somewhat risk-averse," Pomeroy explains. But Van Loan also knew that ECT required major financial resources to continue its strong growth pattern. Consequently, when Dover made its initial overtures, "he was at least willing to consider the idea," Pomeroy says. "He didn't throw my letter in the wastebasket."

The two men later met to discuss the benefits of a Dover acquisition. "I told Dave about the Dover Philosophy, that he could cash out his ownership stake and then, with our capital, go ahead and keep buying companies, running the whole thing as if he still owned it," says Pomeroy. "That got his attention. He really had a vision for this company but was constrained by the financial risk."

As the contracts on the deal were being prepared, Van Loan already was pitching Dover his next planned acquisitions. "I was ecstatic that I would now have the wherewithal to buy really significant companies, and not the small fry I had accumulated," Van Loan says. "I especially had my eye on Luther & Maelzer, a German company focused on the high-volume printed circuit board market, which includes cell phone boards and computer boards. Luther & Maelzer was considered one of the premier bare board testing companies in the world, and I knew it would be an important add-on acquisition for Everett Charles, giving us an expanded global market presence and new market penetration."

Before the Dover acquisition concluded during the week of Thanksgiving 1996, Van Loan was making overtures to Luther & Maelzer's owners about an acquisition. A deal was inked in March 1997. And Van Loan was on a roll: Over the course of the next eight years, he would execute more than a dozen add-on acquisitions, becoming Dover's most active company acquirer. Both ECT and Imaje would help Dover Technologies balance the cyclical fortunes of Universal Instruments through the remainder of the decade and into the new millennium.

The other stand-alone acquisition of 1996 was Tulsa Winch, another company perceived as a platform for future growth. Tulsa Winch was founded in 1929 by a truck salvage operator who utilized the gear sets from the rear axles of Model T trucks to fashion a novel winch. In 1946, the company was sold to Vickers Hydraulics, generating as much as $30 million in sales some years until the fortunes of the oil industry dried up in the 1980s. In 1986, a year in which its sales hovered around $3.5 million, Tulsa Winch was purchased from Vickers in a management buyout led by general manager Ron Hoffman, a manufacturing engineer by training.

When Hoffman initially proposed his idea of buying the company, Vickers management "laughed me out of the room," he recalls. "But I was persistent and went from bank to bank, and was at the point of hocking my house, cars, and retirement accounts when I ran across a fellow who knew a financier that might back me and my partner in the buyout. We hit it off and he became our financial backer. And we bought the company." With Hoffman as president, Tulsa Winch was revitalized. He guided the company into new markets, developed a wealth of new products, and restored the growth that had been lackluster since the 1980s.

By chance, Hoffman had met Tom Reece when Reece was touring the Vickers plant in the early 1980s, a period when Reece was the president of W. C. Norris. In 1995, Hoffman was reading his local newspaper, *Tulsa World*, when he spied a photograph of Reece, who had given a speech the previous day at the University of Tulsa about Dover's acquisition strategy. In the article, Reece had stated that, when Dover buys a stand-alone company, it has no intentions of merging that company with a larger one; allows it to retain its name, employee benefit programs, and management; and does not interfere with its management decisions. But it was Reece's next comment that particularly resonated with Hoffman: "When a company becomes part of Dover, generally we find a business that has quit growing, a small company whose leaders avoid big risks for fear of losing the successful operation they've built. With Dover behind them, they don't see that as such a large risk anymore."

"That really caught my attention," Hoffman says. "We pretty much fit the profile of the company Tom

PAK ON BOARD
Everett Charles Technologies' Bantam-Pak, mounted on a performance board, left, provides reliable testing for the semiconductor industry.

PUMP ACTION
Versatile and dependable, Wilden Pump & Engineering's Advanced metal pump series has bolted construction that ensures total containment of fluid and is made of either die cast aluminum, stainless steel, or alloy C.

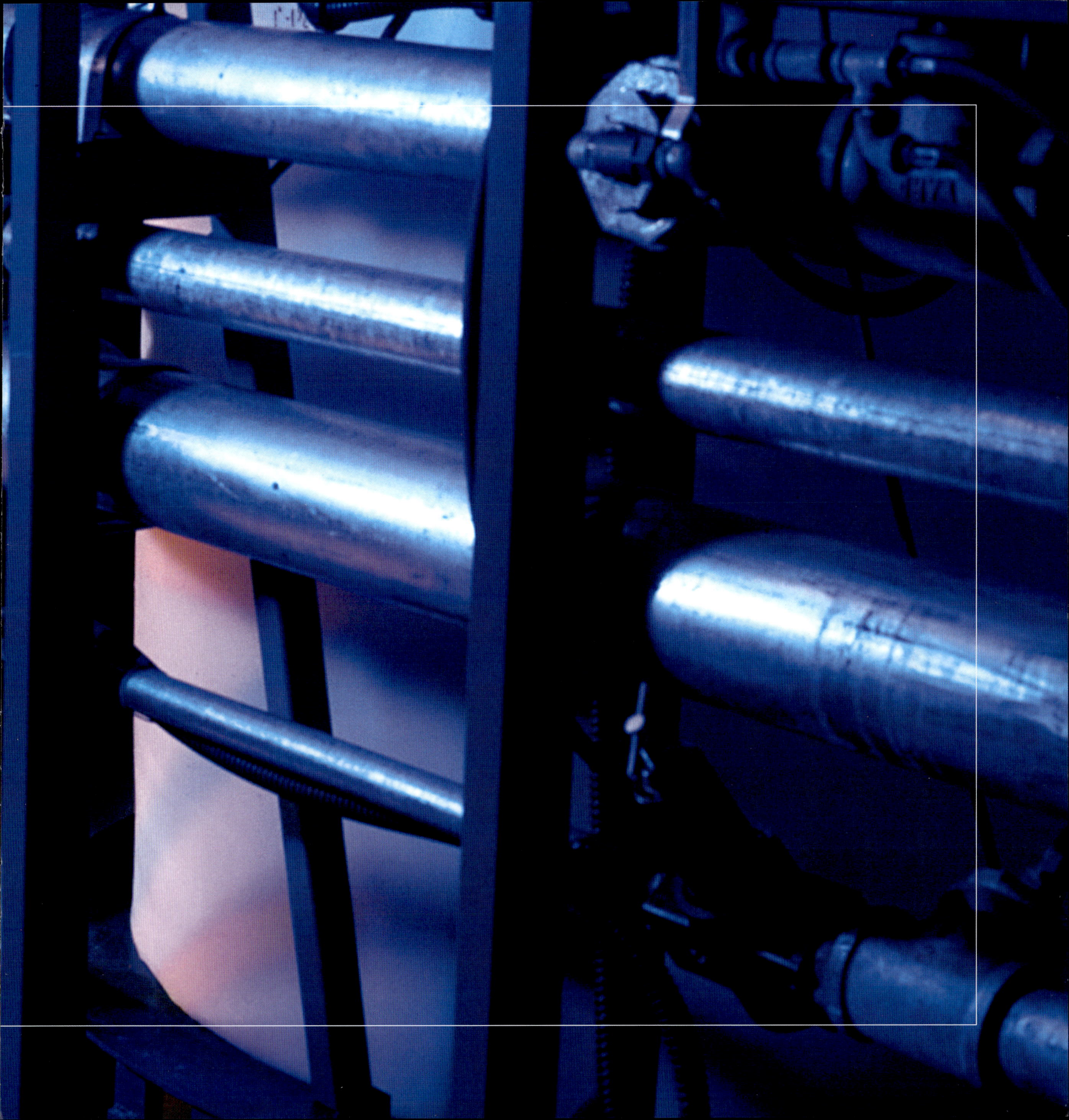

DOVER CORPORATION   TILT TOWARD GROWTH

had described. We needed to grow further, but were constrained by the capital needed." Although small by Dover standards, the acquisition went through. Hoffman would complete three add-on acquisitions at Tulsa Winch from 1996 to 1999, tripling the size of the company.

The acquisition of Tulsa Winch was negotiated by Dover Resources CEO Rudy Herrmann, who became so impressed with Hoffman's managerial capabilities that he asked Hoffman to become his executive vice president in late 1999. Hoffman would succeed Herrmann as Dover Resources CEO in 2002.

Hoffman and Van Loan were far from alone in making add-on acquisitions at Dover's operating companies. From 1994 through 1997, Dover company presidents chalked up an unprecedented thirty-nine add-on acquisitions, among them Soltec's $18 million acquisition of Vitronics, a complementary maker of soldering equipment used in circuit board assembly. The combined company, part of Dover Technologies, was renamed Vitronics Soltec.

The sheer breadth of add-on acquisitions, in addition to the stand-alone acquisitions, changed the face of Dover. By 1998, the corporation comprised more than 150 manufacturing locations, more than 200 product/market niches, and approximately 28,000 employees. "We are not running a single, large race against competition, but hundreds of smaller races simultaneously," Reece commented at the time.

THROUGH MUCK AND MIRE

Dover acquired Wilden Pump & Engineering in 1998. Founded in 1955 by Jim Wilden, the company engineered multiple pumps, including the M-Series, left, which is engaged in a marine application.

INNOVATION: THE WILDEN PUMP

Jim Wilden created an entire industry with his invention of the world's first air-operated, double-diaphragm pump. Today, Wilden Pump & Engineering Company is the world's largest manufacturer of the novel pumps, with more than 50 percent of its sales coming from international markets. The company began when Jim Wilden saw a need for a reliable, lightweight, utilitarian pump that could pump water, slurry, or finely divided substances like cement. The design of Wilden's patented M16 Air Operated Double Diaphragm Pump is simple. The air valve involves only one moving part, yet the product is extremely durable. While a diaphragm on a mechanically driven pump will flex about 500,000 times before breakdown, the diaphragm in the Wilden air-driven pump could flex as many as 30 million times before deteriorating. The pump can move the most viscous fluids from sumps, tanks, and the ground, including ceramics, raw starch, paints and dyes, and pulp for paper.

Not all acquisitions were keepers, however. There would be several divestitures in the mid- to late 1990s, guided by a new divestiture strategy—companies that offered value and financial merit but whose growth was in question. Fitting that profile were Groen's American Metal Ware coffee brewing line, AC Compressor, Bernard Welding, Measurement Systems, and Dieterich Standard, the company from which Gary Roubos had found his way to Dover. "I remember when I sold Dieterich, people said, 'Lew, you've got guts. That's Roubos's company!'" Burns recalls. "But I got a high price for it and was able to show it was not a growth platform company. If a company does not offer a platform for growth and somebody wants to buy it at a good price, we'll consider it. This is a change, but a good one."

Dover would part with another company, representing the largest divestiture in the corporation's history: Dover Elevator International. Initially, Dover planned to spin off the elevator business to shareholders, believing the company did not fit well with Dover's other industrial operations and would grow faster as a separate company. "Our elevator company was the best elevator company in the world from a financial standpoint, but it had come to a point where it had not performed well since the recession of the early 1990s," Reece explains.

"We brought in new management to right the ship, and Dover Elevator gradually restored its historical profit margins," he notes. "But there was some concern at the company that other Dover businesses were becoming more geographically diverse and global, and they wanted the same. We calculated what it would cost to achieve a true global presence, but the price tag—at $1 billion at least—was disconcerting. I told Nigel Davis, the head of Elevator at the time, that maybe globalization is the right thing to do, but it is not the right use of Dover shareholder resources. That's when we discussed the possibility of a spin-off."

DOVER CORPORATION TILT TOWARD GROWTH

> **INNOVATION:** HYDRO SYSTEMS' HYDROGAP EDUCTOR
>
> In 1995, Hydro Systems, which develops units that ensure the safe and correct dilution of cleaning chemicals, unveiled the HydroGap air gap eductor, a patented device that provides the same high level of protection as traditional systems at a fraction of the cost. Chemical dilution units typically hook onto a hose supplying water from a building's water supply. To prevent the chemical from being sucked back into the public water supply in the event of back-siphoning, most units in the marketplace feature so-called Reduced Pressure Zone devices, which cost upward of $100 and require professional installation as well as annual inspection. Hydro Systems developed HydroGap as an alternative, offering the same protection at much lower cost. Initially priced at $25, three new versions of HydroGap air gap eductors cost $6 each. The device does not require external electricity, batteries, pumps, or air pressure; it works from ordinary line pressure available in most buildings.

CROSSING THE PACIFIC
As many of Dover's operating companies worked to become global providers, Dover became a global acquirerer. It started in 1995, when Imaje, a French manufacturer of continuous ink-jet printers, became the first non-United States based Dover operating company. Right: An Imaje promotional piece.

In May 1998, Davis worked with Dover's investment bankers at Goldman Sachs to prepare a road show to meet potential investors interested in an initial public offering of stock. "We were about to set it in motion when Thyssen made an offer we couldn't refuse," Reece says. "Goldman had advised that we could not do any better in the marketplace and, given our fiduciary responsibility to shareholders, we decided to sell the company." In November 1998, Dover sold the company for $1.1 billion to Germany's Thyssen Elevator, a unit of Thyssen Industrie AG.

The sale of Dover Elevator, a company with long, historical ties to the corporation and arguably its best-known brand, was discomfiting for some former executives, including Sutton and Roubos. "I felt it was the right thing to do, but emotionally it was a very difficult thing to do," Roubos says. "The arguments for it were strong, the biggest one being that we were basically a domestic elevator company and the business had become global. To go forward with an international strategy would have required enormous resources and, meanwhile, we would still be competing against competition that was much bigger. But it was a very tough decision to make and hard for many to swallow." Fulfilling the commitment to shareholders, Dover invested virtually all of the after-tax proceeds from the divestiture in its own stock.

As Dover neared the end of the twentieth century, Reece's impact on the corporation was indelible. He had devised and executed a bold strategy for growth without undermining the indispensable tenets of the Dover Philosophy. In Dover's 1997 annual report, Reece avowed, "Decentralization and empowerment are essential. They require corporate managers who select and evaluate rather than direct—and presidents, management teams, and employee groups that like to win and can figure out how." In a 2004 interview, he elaborates: "People here must demonstrate the confidence in really wanting to run their businesses as if they owned them. We give them the autonomy to do that, but trust is a two-way street. We will celebrate the successes with them and be tolerant of the failures caused by factors outside their control. But they must take responsibility for the failures. Those are the kinds of individuals we want running our companies."

With a simple decision in 1997, Reece elevated the critical importance of Dover's operating companies and their independent leadership. For the first time in many years, Dover would report its financial results as seen from the perspective of the operating company presidents, "in shameless emulation of Warren Buffett," Reece noted in his letter to shareholders. But, there were deeper implications at play: The spotlight was shifting from the subsidiaries back to the operating companies. Although subsidiary CEOs still retained the authority to oversee the operating companies and make important stand-alone acquisitions, Reece reaffirmed that the corporation's destiny was in the hands of the operating company presidents. Each had been entrusted to grow his business in an era of profound change and challenge.

Warren Buffett, CEO and chairman of Berkshire Hathaway, wrote a letter to Reece after reading Dover's 1997 annual report: "Tom, I'll make a deal with you. You can shamelessly copy presentations from my letter to shareholders *if* you will let me just as shamelessly copy your operating performance." Known for his refreshing folksiness, Buffett then requested that Reece mail him a few extra copies of Dover's annual report, "so I can send them on to our managers in the spirit of the farmer who entered the henhouse with an ostrich egg and stated, 'I don't like to complain, ladies, but this is just a sample of what the competition is doing.'"

Reece replied, "Dear Warren, Here are a dozen annual reports, as requested. By the way, we think that raising the bar matters, too. Do you know where I can get my hands on a dinosaur egg?"

As Tom Reece and Dover Corporation entered the twenty-first century together, they would find that dinosaur egg.

SHAREHOLDER-'CENTRIC'

Dover's history of candor in financial reporting is exemplified by this 1997 annual report, which was praised by Warren Buffet, the renowned investor and shareholder advocate. This report provided a summary of consolidated income on the basis used internally by the presidents running individual Dover companies in addition to the format required for SEC purposes.

TECHNOBOOM Former CEO Gary Roubos's prescience guiding Dover into the technology sector, and ongoing efforts by CEO Tom Reece to acquire additional technology companies during his tenure at the top, reaped financial rewards in the late 1990s' technology boom. Dover Technologies, the Dover subsidiary composed of the corporation's high-tech and electronic holdings, generated almost half of Dover's sales at the turn of the millennium. Above: Universal Instruments today employs more than 1,000 employees at engineering operations in the U.S., China, and India.

3 LAUNCHING PAD

Fueled by the technology sector, the boom economy of the late 1990s ignited a rocket at Dover Corporation, lifting its earnings per share 34 percent from 1998 to 1999 and another 40 percent in 2000. Much of the boost was provided by Dover's subsidiary that comprised its high-tech and electronic holdings, Dover Technologies. The subsidiary's sales and earnings continued climbing upward at the end of the twentieth century, hesitated for a brief period, and then shot sky-high as the world celebrated a new millennium. Dover's good cheer was shared by many other U.S. corporations: American business had made a comeback as the most competitive performer in the emerging global economy.

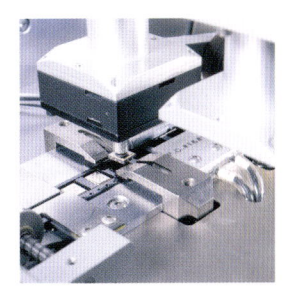

CLEANING UP
Drawing resources from eight factories worldwide, Vectron International boasts a broad array of frequency generation and control products. The photograph depicts a Vectron Class-100 "clean room," where the wafer metallization process takes place.

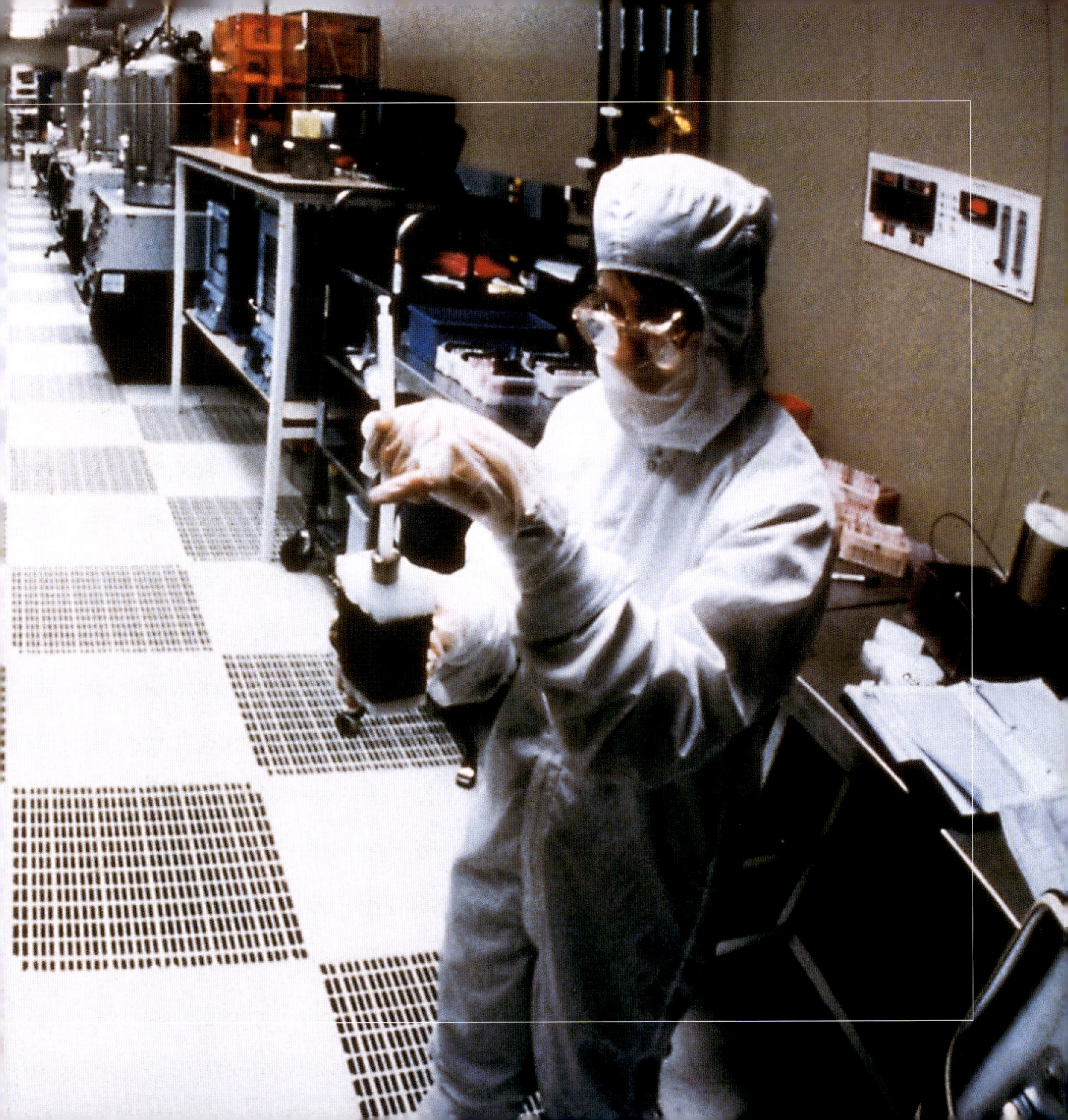

DOVER CORPORATION   LAUNCHING PAD

TESTING BOUNDARIES
ECT's Semiconductor Test Group—a consolidation of several semiconductor test company acquisitions—today makes a variety of sophisticated semiconductor test machines like the one pictured below.

For the first time in history, the galloping Dow Jones stock index thundered past the 10,000 barrier. Unemployment fell to a thirty-year low, and inflation was virtually nonexistent. The United States' economic resurgence was powerful enough to outpace other industrial economies and even played a major role in temporarily eliminating the three-decade-old federal deficit.

It was a remarkable turn-around. Few qualms had characterized the American frame of mind in the 1970s and 1980s as much as listless economic growth, the demoralizing sense that other industrial nations had passed us by, and the fear that American companies had lost their competitive edge in the ruthless global economy. Thanks to aggressive restructuring and the implementation of modern, Internet-based productivity systems for managing capital flows and worldwide supply chains, U.S. corporations were again the envy of the industrial world.

Technology was the locomotive of America's comeback. New products from that industry's brain trust found eager buyers, and new buying patterns emerged as the Internet drew millions of consumers online. The booming technology sector resounded at Dover Technologies, the collection of companies selling specialty electronic components and circuit board assembly and test equipment. The huge upturn in the worldwide electronics industry stimulated a 44 percent increase in the subsidiary's sales to $2 billion from 1999 to 2000, accounting for almost half the sales of the entire corporation that year. The subsidiary's aggregate earnings also soared to new heights in 2000, up 73 percent from the previous year to $392 million.

Surging demand in the telecommunications, data networking, and computer industries had begun to generate higher sales and earnings for several Dover Technologies companies back in 1998. Dover's specialty electronic component manufacturers had expanded their product menus to serve those fast-growing markets, selling the oscillators, transformers, and specialty capacitors that are integral to many wireless and hard-wired communications systems. The pace slowed a bit in 1999, then hurtled forward in 2000, with all eleven companies in Dover Technologies recording higher sales and earnings.

Dover Technologies was not the only Dover subsidiary to enjoy unparalleled returns in 2000. The economic recovery also ushered in dramatic gains for Dover's industrial and commercial businesses: All four Dover subsidiaries—Technologies, Diversified, Resources, and Industries—reported record sales, and three logged record earnings.

A different Dover now met the public. Critical structural changes along with a spate of acquisitions and a few divestitures over the previous ten years had transformed the corporation. Dover's participation in the high-growth electronics industry had increased dramatically; its participation in the low-growth elevator industry had terminated; and its high-growth industrial and commercial activities were expanding. Some subsidiaries swelled overnight into large organizations comprising broad product lines and markets. The aptly named Dover Diversified, for example, listed forty-seven separate businesses operating under its twelve stand-alone companies in 2000.

Despite this organizational metamorphosis, at its core Dover philosophically and culturally remained the same: The values that had served as guideposts for nearly half a century were as visible at the dawn of the twenty-first century as they had been in 1955. "Our basic business proposition—find and acquire financially strong, niche manufacturing businesses that are managed well by people who will stay on and continue to manage them without a lot of corporate oversight—had not changed in the new business climate," says CEO and Chairman Tom Reece. "We were the same Dover, only bigger and stronger."

When Reece became CEO of Dover in May 1994, the corporation listed two companies with sales greater than $100 million—Dover Elevator and Universal Instruments. By 2000, that number had jumped to seventeen, even with the divestiture of Dover Elevator. Overall, since 1997, sales had risen 50 percent and net earnings 70 percent by 2000. Meanwhile, from 1998 through 2000, Dover spent $1.6 billion acquiring a whopping fifty-five companies, forty-six of them add-on acquisitions at the operating company level. "Add-on acquisitions have enabled our companies to reinforce and expand their market niches, move into new

SAFEGUARD

Civacon designs and manufactures equipment for the safe handling and transport of hazardous liquids and dry bulk commodities. Above: A tank trailer outfitted with a Civacon system.

DOVER CORPORATION   LAUNCHING PAD

LEADERSHIP: THE BUILDER

Tom Reece still has the air of the schoolteacher about him. He is passionately interested in everything, from the inner mechanics of Dover's most esoteric products to the recent wave of cultural activities he and his wife, Sandy, have been privileged to attend while living in Manhattan. He reads voraciously, gobbling up books, magazine articles, and nearly impenetrable tracts on cutting-edge manufacturing strategies.

Reece has seamlessly meshed his previous hands-on experience in running three mid-sized Dover manufacturing operations in the heartland of America with the finesse and sophistication needed to run a $5 billion multinational corporation in the nexus of business and industry.

The Reece era at Dover—he stepped down as CEO in December 2004 after more than ten years at the helm but still retains his title as chairman of the board—was one of enormous growth and reinvention. Reece redefined Dover's crucial acquisition strategy to promote an unprecedented volume of add-on acquisitions by the operating companies. He rewrote the corporation's long-term incentive plan for company presidents to stimulate their thinking about synergistic, global acquisitions. He further refined the principles governing stand-alone acquisitions by the subsid-

geographic or product markets, and, because of greater size, attract better management talent," Reece stated in Dover's 2000 annual report.

Roubos and Reece's undaunted "Tilt Toward Growth" strategy was on a roll. Accretive acquisitions since 1998 included Sargent Controls' purchase of Sonic Industries, the largest supplier of aerospace specialty fasteners to Boeing, and a market leader in the manufacture of standard and special bolts for aircraft engines and other applications; Universal's acquisition of Alphasem, a leading Swiss manufacturer of semiconductor equipment; and Everett Charles Technologies' acquisition of five separate companies within the first two years of joining Dover. As these examples illustrate, operating company presidents were engineering acquisitions for strategic reasons: to expand internationally, gain market share, penetrate new markets, add product lines, enlarge customer bases, or gain economies of scale.

While company presidents were flexing their entrepreneurial muscles and bulking up their organizations, subsidiary CEOs were doing much the same. Dover had tallied four stand-alone acquisitions in 1998, all of them market leaders: PDQ, the top manufacturer of touchless car-washing equipment in the United States; Wiseco Piston, the leading domestic producer

iaries, adding to Dover's customary criteria of solid growth, market leadership, and management excellence the requirement that candidates be a "platform" company upon which further acquisitions would be made.

Reece's talents were obvious to Dover executives early on. Tapped to lead Ronningen-Petter at the age of twenty-eight—the youngest company president in Dover's history—Reece did well enough at Ronningen-Petter to be transferred in 1978 to DE-STA-CO, a Detroit-based manufacturer then in need of more modern management. In 1983, he was transferred to W. C. Norris in Tulsa, Oklahoma, and guided its restructuring as the company sought to cope with drastically reduced demand for its equipment. A year and one-half later, Gary Roubos, Dover's CEO at the time, proposed another transfer to Reece, this time to head Universal Instruments in Binghamton, New York. Reece knew Universal was poised to become Dover's premier company, but he turned Roubos down.

"Gary was in a bind and I wanted to be the good soldier, but I decided to fulfill a commitment I had made to my wife, that we would stay put in Tulsa until our daughters graduated from high school," he explains. "I could not let my family down. At a lot of other corporations, if you're offered a job and don't take it, you're gone. But Gary respected how much my family meant to me."

The girls graduated in Tulsa. And Roubos tagged Reece as his successor.

GROWING GAINS

Dover Chairman Tom Reece earned his way to the top by presiding over three Dover operating companies and heading Dover Resources. Because of his past experience, he knew firsthand the importance of maintaining autonomous operating company management.

---

of high-performance pistons used in racing engines for cars, motorcycles, boats, and snowmobiles; Quartzdyne, the world's top designer and producer of quartz-based pressure transducers used primarily in gas and oil drilling; and Wilden Pump and Engineering, the leader by a substantial margin in its niche of the worldwide pump market. Wilden was Dover's largest acquisition at the time it was acquired in 1998. The corporation paid about $250 million for the company, roughly 45 percent of the $554 million Dover invested in the purchase of new businesses that year.

Wilden Pump and Wiseco were both created by plucky, innovative men with a streak of entrepreneurialism. Clyde Wiseman, founder of Wiseco in 1941, wanted to make his speedboat go faster, so he forged his own pistons to boost acceleration. He set up Wiseco in an Ohio garage, and it soon became the after-market leader in performance forged pistons. Jim Wilden, founder of Wilden Pump in 1955, was the inventor of a revolutionary air-operated, double-diaphragm pump, used by multiple industries to move diverse fluids safely and efficiently. The company operated initially out of a corrugated metal building in the middle of a California walnut grove owned by the Wilden family. Both companies would prove important contributors to Dover's future growth.

DOVER CORPORATION   LAUNCHING PAD

FULL SPEED AHEAD
Wiseco, a PMI company, continually works to develop the industry's highest-performing and most reliable pistons. On the road or racetrack, Wiseco pistons are the premium choice. Above: Racer Chris Carr (leading the pack) has made the Wiseco choice.

INNOVATION: WISECO'S PRECISION FORGE PROCESS

A company does not become the leading domestic producer of high-performance pistons in racing engines for cars, motorcycles, boats, and snowmobiles without a few innovations along the way. Wiseco—a world-class manufacturer of high-performance, forged pistons for the snowmobile, motorcycle, ATV, personal watercraft, outboard marine, and automotive markets—bases its success, in part, on a novel forging method. Wiseco's Precision Forge Process assists the forging of materials into intricate shapes, offering the strongest possible part with far less waste and machining. Not only are the forgings lighter, they offer superior ductility, strength, and resistance to impact and fatigue. Forging has been at the center of Wiseco since its founder, Clyde Wiseman, set up Wiseco in an Ohio garage. Within a short time, Wiseco emerged as the leader in the performance forged pistons after-market.

Jim Wilden had met Tom Reece for lunch in the mid-1980s to discuss the possible sale of his company to Dover. Although Wilden changed his mind about selling, he and Reece kept in touch over the years. After Wilden's death in 1989, his wife and daughters took the reins at the family firm, strengthening its operating management and unveiling several new products, such as a Teflon-composite double-diaphragm pump.

"While Jim was alive, he wasn't willing to sell his business, but he always said that, if Wilden Pump were sold, Dover would be the company that he wanted to entrust his organization and his company's reputation to," Reece comments. "When his family was ready to sell, they remembered Jim's wishes." Wilden Pump perfectly fit the Dover model for a stand-alone acquisition: high-margin business, much of it global; superior innovation and entrepreneurship; unparalleled brand equity and first-class distribution; a good, strong management team that remains in place; and substantial foreign sales.

The Wiseco acquisition was negotiated by Jerry Yochum, CEO of Dover Diversified. "I used to race motorcycles and had known about Wiseco for about twenty years," Yochum says. "My son also was a motorcycle racer—I used to 'wrench' for him—and we both were frequent users of their products. So, when it came on the market—some of the owners were approaching retirement and wished to monetize the equity they'd built up—I had this unusual background that proved valuable in negotiating the deal."

Reece was initially unconvinced about the Wiseco acquisition. "I felt it was too retail- and consumer-oriented—basically not an industrial company," he explains. "But Jerry was very strong in his arguments, and he understood this company and market extremely well; so, we convinced ourselves it had the trappings of an industrial company.

PISTON PROTECTION

A piston is the first line of defense against the extreme heat and pressures of an internal combustion engine. Superior sealing, reliability, and tight clearances are of the utmost importance in safely creating horsepower. Wiseco's Piston Kit offers this assurance.

DOVER CORPORATION LAUNCHING PAD

THE SOFT TOUCH

PDQ Manufacturing, headquartered just outside Green Bay in DePere, Wisconsin, boasts the industry's leading touch-free vehicle wash research and development team, as well as state-of-the-art assembly facilities. Above: Skilled production is orchestrated utilizing the latest in lean manufacturing practices.

Besides, we felt it was a good platform company: There were all these small, single-product companies out there in the performance motor-sports industry that might be an acquisition play for us." Four months after the deal closed, Wiseco made its first add-on acquisition.

The Wiseco acquisition suited the parameters of Dover's emerging growth platform concept for stand-alone acquisitions. Although the corporation referred to the *platform concept* for the first time in 1996 when it acquired both Everett Charles Technologies and Tulsa Winch, earlier acquisitions such as Heil, Hill PHOENIX, and Imaje also met the criteria of a platform company. Even veteran Dover companies such as Rotary Lift, Sargent Controls, and the two OPW companies had carried out numerous add-on acquisitions over the years.

In effect, Dover did not initiate the platform concept as much as evolve it, refining the principles through the years. "There is no absolute line in the sand regarding platforms and non-platforms," Reece explains.

"There is no decision point that says 'non-platforms yesterday and only platforms tomorrow.' There was just this recognition that certain companies we owned, and some that we had acquired, had the market presence and position to be good candidates for expansion through both internal development and add-on acquisitions," he adds. "So, part of the strategic shift at the end of the 1990s was identifying companies that we already owned that were platforms for expansionary investment, as well as redefining our thinking in terms of future stand-alone acquisitions." The new "thinking" was to focus on companies that were much larger than Dover's previous targets, more global in their view of business, and more international in their management depth.

Those criteria marked a departure from the corporation's customary standards for acquiring stand-alone companies. In the 1970s and 1980s, Dover typically acquired small to mid-sized manufacturing companies priced between $25 million and $50 million and possessing the traditional Dover attributes of having niche products, market leadership, pretax margins between 15 and 20 percent, after-tax returns on investment exceeding 25 percent, and top-flight management that would stay on to run the business post-acquisition. In most cases, Dover acquired only companies that owned tangible manufacturing assets.

However, few of those companies were global organizations, and most lacked experienced international management to build a sustainable global presence. "We learned some tough lessons from several low-growth companies we had acquired that ended up divestitures," says Vice President of Corporate Development Bob Tyre. "In these cases, we had failed to question whether or not the company's management had a viable plan for growing the business. As we say here, 'It's a bitch when the niche falls in the ditch.'"

The revamped platform strategy directed subsidiary CEOs to target larger companies in which Dover could invest its excess cash flow to achieve significant earnings growth, funding both internal growth objectives and strategic add-on acquisitions. Candidates also must possess superior intellectual capital—internationally experienced management at all levels within their organizations. The companies must serve global markets or at least be thinking in that direction. And, finally, they must be valued as much for their intangible assets, such as strong brand name, intellectual property, and patents, as for their tangible manufacturing assets. "Increasingly, the value-added comes from things like engineering, a strong channel to market, excellent customer service, and sophisticated supply-chain management," Tyre explains. "The latter is especially important because centers of expertise in low-cost manufacturing are continually moving around in the global manufacturing environment, from Mexico to China one day, to India and Vietnam the next."

As the corporation hammered together the new planks in the platform strategy, its procedures

"PART OF THE STRATEGIC SHIFT AT THE END OF THE 1990S WAS IDENTIFYING COMPANIES THAT WE ALREADY OWNED THAT WERE PLATFORMS FOR EXPANSIONARY INVESTMENT, AS WELL AS REDEFINING OUR THINKING IN TERMS OF FUTURE STAND-ALONE ACQUISITIONS."

— Tom Reece, Dover Corporation CEO (1994–2004)

SWEP AWAY
SWEP International in 2002 was separated from Tranter PHE and formed into a Dover operating company. A Sweden-based company, it is the biggest manufacturer of compact brazed heat exchangers, above.

CULTURE: ACQUIRING

George Ohrstrom is the father of Dover's time-honored acquisition strategy: to seek and buy small, family-owned or closely held companies that make highly specialized products for national markets in which they are the recognized leaders. Such companies typically do not sell products retail, generally hold the patents on their technologies, and are dependably profitable; they are not in a "turn-around" situation. They also boast a capable management team eager to stay on and manage their companies after the deal closes. The four companies that combined to become Dover Corporation in 1955 shared those general characteristics, though they manufactured different products for dissimilar markets.

Over the past fifty years, this acquisition strategy has remained largely intact, culminating in the diversified portfolio of independent companies comprising Dover today. The corporation's first two CEOs and first two acquisition specialists, by and large, continued to target small, family-owned manufacturing concerns fitting the Ohrstrom model.

Acquisitions outside the fold have been the exception and not the rule at Dover. The first significant foray from convention was Universal Instruments in 1979, a public company that made products for the nascent technology sector and cost substantially more to acquire than Dover's previous acquisitions had. The acquisition of Universal sent a message that Dover would entertain larger, more expensive companies outside the sphere of traditional "metal-bashing" manufacturing; and, over the next twenty-five years, Dover would acquire numerous Information Age companies, aggregating them under the Dover Technologies umbrella.

Further changes in acquisition practices got underway during the term of CEO Gary Roubos. When the Dover subsidiaries were formed in the late 1980s, the new heads of those organizations were granted the authority to acquire stand-alone companies, as long as the candidates fit the Ohrstrom model and met exacting financial criteria: a 25 percent after-tax return on investment, 15 percent pretax profit margin, and 10 percent pretax income growth. Near the end of Roubos's term, a new compensation matrix for Dover executives helped fuel several acquisitions of stand-alone companies as well as abundant add-on acquisitions by the operating company presidents.

It was not until the "Tilt Toward Growth" strategy kicked into gear during the term of Dover's fourth CEO, Tom Reece, that the corporation's acquisition strategy broadened beyond the boundaries established by Ohrstrom. At that time, in the mid-1990s, the subsidiaries and operating companies were not making nearly enough acquisitions to provide the growth Dover required to sustain its customary shareholder returns.

In 2003, Reece and Tyre also refined the criteria for making stand-alone acquisitions. The new growth platform concept targeted the acquisition of much larger, global companies with internationally experienced management, strong brand names, intellectual property, and patents. Such companies must meet another criterion: They must have the ability to distinguish themselves from competitors and maintain that advantage over time. Reece called the strategy "defensible differentiation."

After the recession years of 2001 and 2002, Reece and Tyre also fine-tuned the add-on acquisition criteria, mandating new "threshold requirements" that included a minimum 15 to 20 percent internal rate of return, stronger due diligence by company presidents, and an overview of integration challenges prior to acquiring a company. During the Reece era, from 1994 to 2005, Dover invested more than $3 billion in more than 165 stand-alone and add-on acquisitions.

The corporation also made one other relatively recent change to the Ohrstrom model: the relaxation of its standards to permit the purchase of "turn-around" companies that have great brand names but have fallen upon hard times. In this regard certainly, George Ohrstrom might have raised a skeptical eyebrow. But, given the astonishing growth of the small corporation he founded fifty years ago, he would have little to bicker about.

for acquiring stand-alone companies required some adjustment. To buy larger companies—organizations that were more sophisticated in the acquisition process and, therefore, had clearer views of their market values—Dover, in some cases, needed to participate in auctions led by investment banks in which it bid against both customary peers and private equity groups. The competition to buy large, attractive, stand-alone companies was cut-throat; and Dover would find only a few suitable candidates meeting its criteria. "We want to increase the number of platform acquisitions as a percent of our portfolio but realize we often have to stretch a bit to get them," Tyre concedes.

Not all extant Dover operating companies were viewed as platform companies. Those serving very narrow specialty markets continued to be operated as before with their focus more on internal growth policies than external investments in add-on acquisitions. Nevertheless, several operating companies would evolve into broad-based platforms. Wiseco, for example, acquired six complementary businesses through 2003, a prized, global collection of performance motor-sports companies that included: Prox Inter BV, an Amsterdam-based supplier of cast pistons; U.S.-based JE Piston, a leader in high-performance pistons for the automotive aftermarket; Vertex Pistons, an Italian maker of cast-aluminum pistons for two-cycle engine applications; Carillo Industries, the premier maker of steel connecting rods for performance automotive and motorcycle markets; Perfect Bore Limited, a United Kingdom manufacturer of thin-walled, coated cylinder liners and specialty pistons for racing; and France's Chambon S.A., a leader in automotive crankshafts primarily for European racing markets.

Those companies combined with Wiseco to form Performance Motorsports, Inc., the umbrella name for that growth platform. Although from an operational perspective the companies reside within PMI, they retain their individual brand names, each highly recognizable in the marketplace. "Jerry Yochum was the visionary here, followed by Jim Johnson," says Reece. Johnson is the president of PMI and a former executive at Cummins Engine, the world's largest producer of diesel engines above two hundred horsepower. "Jerry had the vision to build the platform, and Jim executed the deals," he adds. "They've built Wiseco from a $20 million company into a $100 million one with truly global reach and more acquisitions to come."

Other operating companies' add-on programs also were in high gear in the new millennium. Reece had challenged company presidents to be more aggressive in making acquisitions, and they had met his terms: Of the twenty-three acquisitions Dover engineered in 2000, twenty-one were synergistic, or strategic, add-ons or product-line additions that were folded into the acquiring operating company.

"We expect our presidents to run their companies as if they own them, and that is a powerful tool for focusing top management attention," Reece asserts. Indeed, many presidents would guide their companies into the new millennium with entrepreneurial gusto. Rotary Lift set company records for sales and profits in 2000,

CRANKING UP THE HEAT

Performance Motorsports, Inc., acquired St. Etienne, France–based Chambon S.A. in December 2002. Chambon augments PMI's power cell portfolio with its capability to produce high-quality crankshafts, below, manufactured from both billet and forged steel.

DOVER CORPORATION LAUNCHING PAD

AUTONOMY: PMI

Dover's Performance Motorsports, Inc., gathered momentum with the corporation's 1998 purchase of Wiseco Piston, the second-leading domestic producer of high-performance pistons used in racing engines for cars, motorcycles, boats, and snowmobiles. Since executing that platform acquisition, the corporation has burned rubber around the world, assembling a formidable group of performance motor-sports equipment suppliers—a textbook example of the ability of a platform company to grow quickly by being a part of Dover.

Within six months of joining Dover, Wiseco's management jump-started the rollout with the acquisition of Prox Inter BV, an Amsterdam-based supplier of aftermarket cast pistons, rod kits, bearings, and clutch plates. Next up on the acquisition express was Huntington Beach, California—based JE Pistons, the market leader for high-performance automotive pistons, giving Wiseco an even stronger base to service that market. Wiseco is revered by motorcyclists for its performance pistons, rings, pins, and components, engineered for off-road motorbikes, street bikes, and the full gamut of Harley-Davidsons. At that juncture, in June 1999, Dover formed PMI to "house" the three performance motor-sports companies from an operational perspective, although each retains its autonomous management and highly recognizable brand name.

PMI made its first acquisition with Vertex Pistons. Based in Reggio Emilia, Italy, it is a manufacturer of cast-aluminum pistons for two-cycle engine applications and was part of a lawn and gardening equipment group of companies. The owners decided to separate the piston business from the rest and sold to Dover in September 2000. Vertex was followed into PMI by three more companies: Carillo Industries of San Clemente, California, the premier maker of steel connecting rods for performance automotive and motorcycle markets; Perfect Bore Limited of the United Kingdom, a manufacturer of thin-walled, coated cylinder liners and specialty pistons for racing; and Chambon S.A., a French company considered a leader in automotive crankshafts primarily in the European racing markets. Although each of the companies within PMI are operated autonomously, they are bound by a common strategy and an intense focus on serving customer needs in the performance aftermarket.

The PMI story provides an excellent example of how a focused management group with a clear strategy was able to build a platform comprised of complementary businesses offering system solutions to a growing customer base. Given the extensive skill base across PMI companies, the opportunity exists to jointly develop a highly engineered power cell including cylinder line, piston, and connecting rod. As they say in auto racing, PMI is in the "groove," the fastest lane of the track. Vrooom!

PISTON-PACKING POWER
JE Pistons was one of the first PMI acquisitions. Based in Huntington Beach, California, JE Pistons earned the number one position in the United States for high-performance pistons in the automotive powersports aftermarket, above.

primarily through two acquisitions: Forward Manufacturing, whose proprietary two-post lift design reaches end users through a distribution channel different from Rotary Lift's; and the Advantage product line, which provides parallelogram lifts and expanded Rotary's heavy-duty product range. Heil Environmental became Dover's fifth-largest earner in 2000, thanks, in part, to a decision by major waste haulers to update their garbage truck fleets after several years of neglect. That same year, Hill PHOENIX acquired a new production facility in Brazil, opened a new branch operations center in the southeastern United States, and added walk-in coolers to its refrigeration product line with the acquisition of National Cooler. Many other companies displayed similar zeal.

"The most important job is that of the operating company president," Reece affirms. "We expect people to operate effectively, and we emphasize mutual trust." This decades-old philosophy would continue to sustain Dover through the cyclical ups and downs of the marketplace.

The year 2001 marked an abrupt turn of this cycle and a sharp reversal of fortune for Dover. The vigorous technology sector, which had contributed nearly half the corporation's sales in 2000, unexpectedly plunged into lethargy, followed a couple quarters hence by a recession that unsettled the industrial markets served by a number of Dover's other subsidiaries. "We started seeing real trouble in the last quarter of 2000 when volume levels started to tail off in the circuit board

WALK RIGHT IN
Hill PHOENIX entered the walk-in refrigeration market in 1999 by building a variety of custom and specialty display systems, like the one seen below, and by acquiring the National Cooler Company in San Dimas, California.

DOVER CORPORATION   LAUNCHING PAD

assembly and test equipment market," Reece recalls. "We had just put out our biggest quarterly earnings ever in October when the analysts realized the 'book-to-bill' at Universal was negative, and the stock value went down. We followed the bookings at Universal very closely; and, when they didn't improve, I wrote an e-mail to company presidents and subsidiary CEOs, saying I didn't feel very good about the economy and we'd better be watching our belts."

Scant weeks later, the dot-com bubble floating many technology stocks finally popped, drenching the turbulent sector in red ink. Sales and bookings at Dover Technologies tumbled to a fraction of the numbers reported a year earlier, and profits vanished. Dover previously had committed capital to expanding production capacity at several Dover Technologies companies and, in the case of Universal Instruments, was dusting off a new multimillion dollar facility in Binghamton, New York, when the crash hit. The extra capacity was surplus now, and Universal was forced to downsize to meet the changed reality of the marketplace.

In the second half of 2001, the economic malaise further swamped Dover's specialty electronic component companies. Vectron's biggest customer, Lucent, sharply curtailed its purchasing as its sales volume sank, stranding Vectron with inventory but few orders. "Vectron had grown like a weed during the bubble, and then fell real hard post-bubble," Tyre says. "Some of its add-on acquisitions turned out well; others did not. We've right-sized the business now, and it is a successful survivor."

Reece had endured cyclical upheaval in the early 1980s, first as president of DE-STA-CO in Detroit and then as president of petroleum equipment supplier W. C. Norris. He was pragmatic about the market challenges. "People ask me why Dover exposed itself to the cyclicality of the electronics industry. My feeling then and now is that this segment may be more cyclical than the other businesses we're in; but, by the same token, it is a major

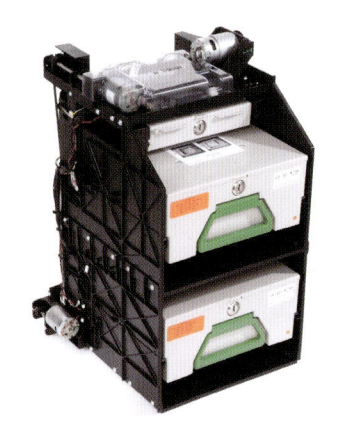

INNOVATION: THE TRITON DISPENSING MECHANISM

As a fully integrated manufacturer, Triton leads the industry in its ability to manufacture innovative and profitable cash-dispensing automatic teller machines for off-premise locations. The company's breakthrough Triton Dispensing Mechanism (TDM) was unveiled in 2002 and quickly took the market by storm, representing a key milestone in Triton's efforts to serve its cost-conscious and profit-minded customers. Thanks to an integrated design that utilizes plastic to combine and consolidate the part count, overall assembly time and part cost are substantially pared. The TDM line presents minimal ongoing maintenance and service needs, making it the best low-cost ATM on the market. Added to these features are state-of-the-art electronics, a locking cassette, and automatic error recovery to maximize uptime.

"ELECTRONICS IS AS FUNDAMENTAL TO THE U.S. AND WORLD ECONOMIES AS OIL AND GAS, AND IS EXPECTED TO GROW FASTER THAN GDP FOR MANY YEARS TO COME. WE HAVE TO PUT UP WITH VOLATILITY; BUT, IF YOU ARE POSITIONED RIGHT— AS I BELIEVE WE ARE—YOU CAN EXPECT LONG-TERM GROWTH PROSPECTS."

— Tom Reece, Dover Corporation Chairman of the Board (1999–present)

industry with a long-term bias for growth. Electronics is as fundamental to the U.S. and world economies as oil and gas, and is expected to grow faster than GDP for many years to come. We have to put up with volatility; but, if you are positioned right—as I believe we are—you can expect long-term growth prospects."

The financial distress consuming Dover Technologies took a toll on the corporation's 2001 sales and earnings, which declined from 2000 by 14 percent to $4.2 billion and 64 percent to $170.2 million, respectively. All four subsidiaries reported lower earnings, although some operating companies fared better than others, and two subsidiaries—Dover Diversified and Dover Resources—reported higher sales.

Throughout the ordeal, Dover company presidents operated with characteristic initiative and grit. Although compelled to cut costs, they maintained a long-term

WHERE THE MONEY IS

As the leading provider of off-premise ATMs, Triton is committed to redefining the retail market for cash delivery systems. Acquired in 2000, Triton is the second largest manufacturer of ATMs in the United States, boasting more than 100,000 installations in seventeen countries worldwide.

focus and continued to invest in internal product-development plans while pruning cost elsewhere. "I credit our operating companies with handling the magnitude of the volatility well," Reece says. "They managed to ramp up production quickly in the up-cycle to create real value without building in excessive cost, and then downsized appropriately to meet the challenges of the moment. As a result, they were primed to achieve solid gains when the markets turned upwards again."

The corporation had ridden out other market downturns, including the collapse of the petroleum market in the 1980s and the impact of globalization on manufacturing in the 1990s. In both cases, operating companies had refused to sacrifice long-term growth for a quick fix. Rather, they had struck a balance between cutting expenses and investing for future gains by modernizing their manufacturing methods, rethinking their sales and marketing operations, developing new products, and making add-on acquisitions. The exigencies of globalization, for example, had

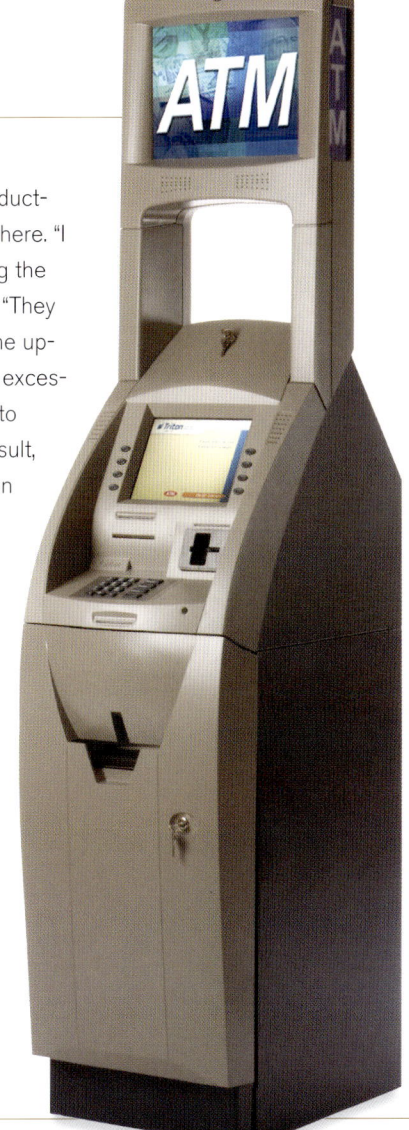

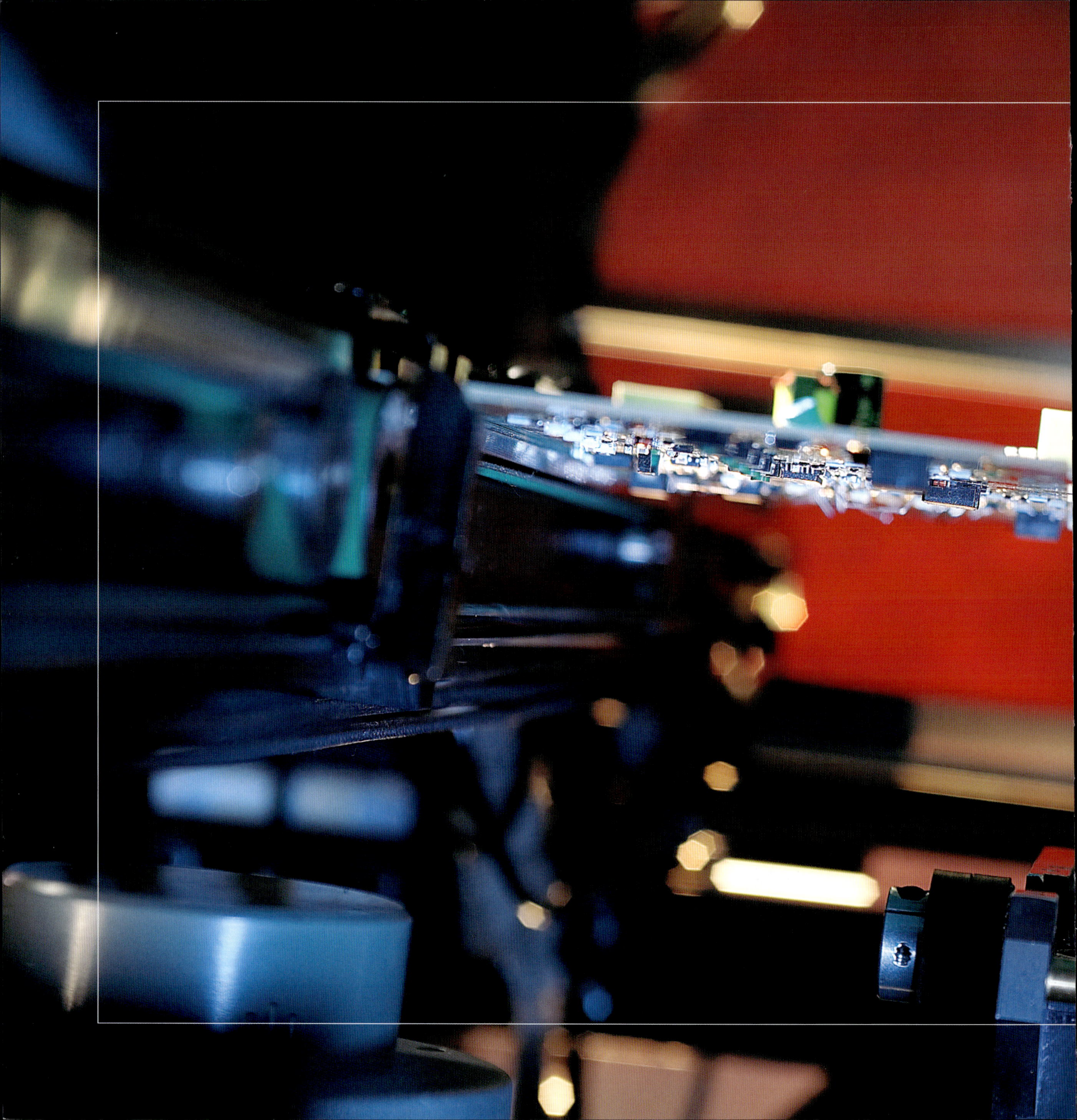

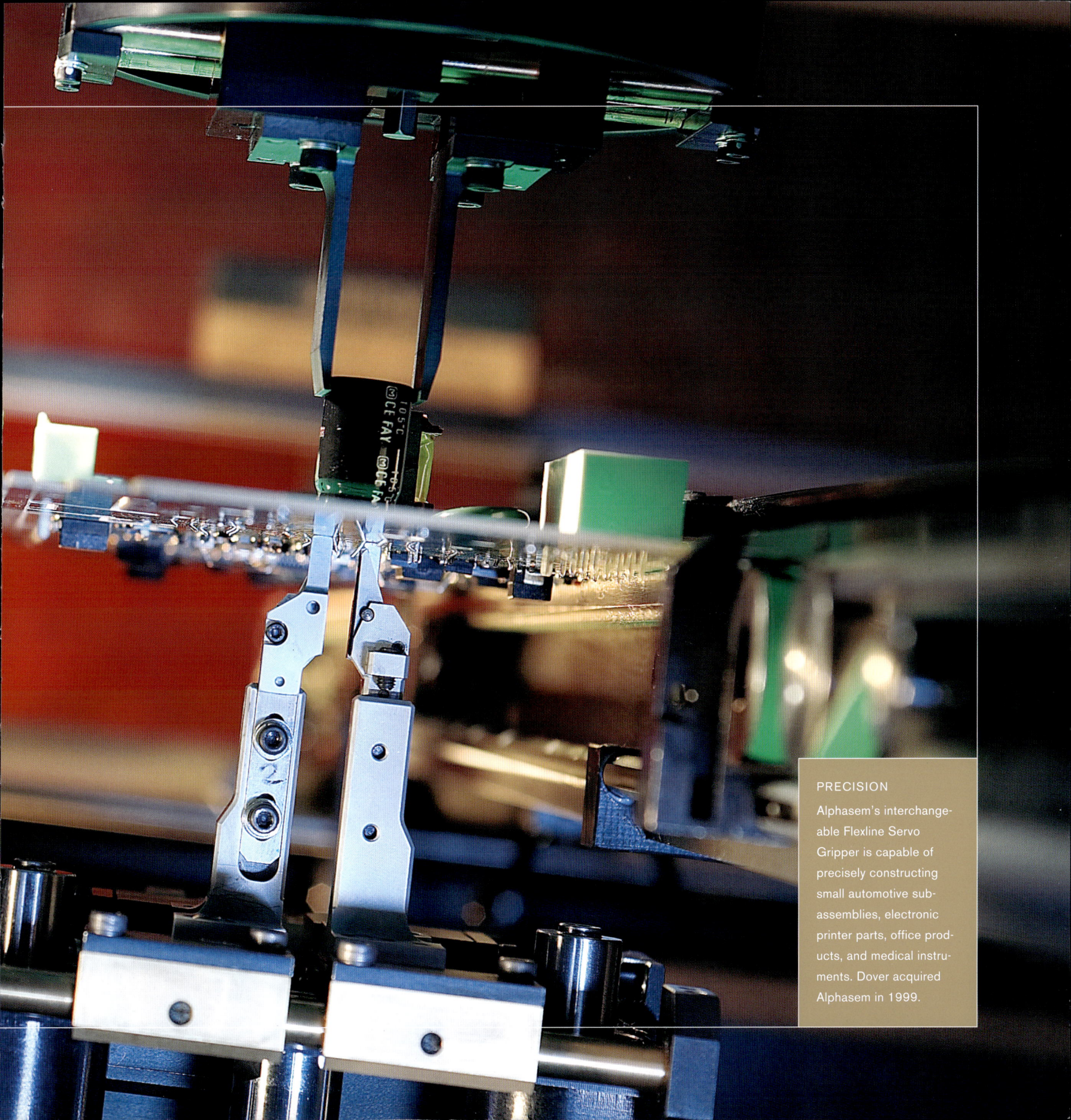

PRECISION
Alphasem's interchangeable Flexline Servo Gripper is capable of precisely constructing small automotive subassemblies, electronic printer parts, office products, and medical instruments. Dover acquired Alphasem in 1999.

DOVER CORPORATION LAUNCHING PAD

INNOVATION: VITRONICS SOLTEC'S SELECTIVE SOLDERING

Founded in 1916 as a designer of soldering tools, Vitronics Soltec has continually pushed the envelope on new soldering techniques. This global manufacturer of wave and reflow soldering and curing equipment for the electronics industry introduced a major new technology in the 1990s: Selective Soldering, for which it earned two U.S. patents. The technology involved the application of solder to preselected parts of a printed circuit board, as opposed to the prior technology in which the entire circuit board received the same process treatment. The ability to solder specific parts on a circuit board gives board designers more flexibility with respect to board layout, as well as increased use of low-cost components. Today, Vitronics Soltec specializes in the development and manufacturing of mass soldering systems for the circuit board assembly industry, developing leading platforms that cover all three mainstream soldering technologies: Wave, Reflow, and Selective Soldering.

SURE ENOUGH

In 2000, Civacon, part of OPW Fluid Transfer Group, acquired Sure Seal, a manufacturer of patented butterfly valves, ball valves, sampling systems, actuators, and hopper tees, like the one shown, right.

compelled many Dover companies to focus on making their manufacturing and other processes more efficient and on improving their service to customers. Company presidents have engaged in continuous improvement programs ever since, deploying such techniques as focused factories, cellular manufacturing, and Six Sigma to lower costs, shorten lead times, reduce inventories, improve product quality, or improve customer access to the products they want when they want them.

To underscore the importance of that continuing effort, in 2001 Reece buffed up a slogan he had first used as president of DE-STA-CO: "Doing the Right Things Right." The maxim encouraged company presidents to implement well thought-out strategies and tactics readying their companies for vigorous growth when markets revived. Several operating companies took the program to heart, investing Dover capital in strategic alliances with suppliers, foreign manufacturing and sales facilities, and myriad customer-focused strategies. Each company did its own "thing," culminating in a burst of activity that belied the severity of the market depression.

Hill PHOENIX, for example, recruited several seasoned executives, who applied their previous experiences with cost-reduction and process-improvement strategies to the company's ongoing efforts to enhance

LEAN MACHINES

Emboldened by Dover's "Doing the Right Things Right" program, Heil Environmental was but one of many Dover companies in the new millennium embracing lean manufacturing techniques in their plants and assembly operations. Left: Heil workers using Kaizen improvement methods.

productivity. The executives examined each business and manufacturing process, starting with the design of a product, and then benchmarked those processes against the best in other industries. New campaigns emerged from this analysis. For instance, by partnering with suppliers to deliver parts and materials "just in time" from consigned inventory in space leased to suppliers within Hill PHOENIX facilities, the company was able to substantially reduce both costs and lead times.

Several companies invested in new product development that anticipated their customers' needs, such as OPW Fueling Components, which developed PISCES, a system that prevents leaks between underground storage tanks and fuel pumps, a source of major environmental concern. The company's engineers eliminated the leaks that typically developed around rigid joints, offering an environmentally friendly solution to its customers' evolving needs. Rotary Lift, meanwhile, developed its new in-bay automotive lift, which incorporates advanced computer technology right into the lift. The system enables an automotive technician, without ever leaving his or her post, to instantly access information about a vehicle make, model, or component, as well as instructions on repairs and warranty information.

Other companies expanded their presence in global markets. Universal Instruments, which drew half its revenue from Asia at the onset of the new millennium and had long deployed a direct sales staff there to remain close to its customers, concluded that the market dynamics required local manufacturing in Asia. With Dover

DOVER CORPORATION LAUNCHING PAD

A-OK ACQUISITION

In 2000, Dover acquired OK International, which had evolved from its origins in 1946 as a specialist machining operation into a leading Silicon Valley–based global supplier of tools and equipment for the electronics workbench, printed circuit board assembly, and repair and rework industries. The company's products are sold through wholly owned international subsidiaries. Right: A hand-soldering unit manufactured by Metcal, an OK International business.

capital, the company established manufacturing and engineering facilities in China to make flexible chip-placement equipment for both international original-equipment manufacturers and contract electronics manufacturers.

Eleven companies in all invested Dover capital in add-on acquisitions in 2001. Having discovered that its customers wanted coding not only on their products but also on the external packaging, Imaje met that need by acquiring Markpoint Holding, a Swedish company that put coding on cartons and pallets. Similar efforts were in place at many other Dover companies. All were guided by Dover's enduring business philosophy: "Perceive customers' real needs, and provide products and services to meet or exceed them; provide better products and services than competitors; invest to maintain competitive advantage; and expect a fair price for the extra value we add.... Success demands a constant focus on product quality and innovation and exceptional customer service."

The year 2002 unfortunately echoed the difficult conditions of 2001. While many operating companies extended their market leadership and strengthened their margins, slowly recovering markets suddenly weakened during the second half of the year, causing Dover's sales to fall 4 percent below the 2001 level to $4.1 billion. For the first time in Dover's history, the corporation did not report net earnings, posting instead a net loss of $121 million. The doleful market conditions were a factor but not the only culprit: Dover had adopted governmentally mandated new accounting practices that resulted in a significant impairment charge to equity.

The severe depression in the electronics segment worsened in 2002. Dover Technologies reported a 13 percent decline in sales and a loss of $29 million as compared to earnings of $5.8 million the previous year, and its record earnings of $383 million in 2000. That year, Dover Technologies had accounted for nearly half Dover's sales; in 2002, that figure had been sheared to approximately 25 percent. To curtail expenses, the circuit board assembly and test (CBAT) businesses and the specialty electronics component (SEC) businesses slimmed their workforces by 15 percent and 13 percent, respectively. Several companies also reduced their capacity to adapt to the current market opportunities. "The companies did whatever they could to become profitable, from cutting back to completely restructuring," says John Pomeroy, Dover Technologies CEO.

The most significant change was the geographic shift of several CBAT and SEC operating companies to Asia, with an emphasis on China, the strongest of the telecommunications equipment markets. By the end of 2003, nearly all the CBAT businesses were manufacturing in China, either at their own facilities or through subcontractors; and several SEC companies had opened Asian-based sales offices and, in certain cases, manufacturing facilities.

As he had in 2001, Reece remained sanguine that "doing things right" would right the foundering ship when markets improved.

While the operating companies confronted the exigencies of the market downturn, Dover's corporate

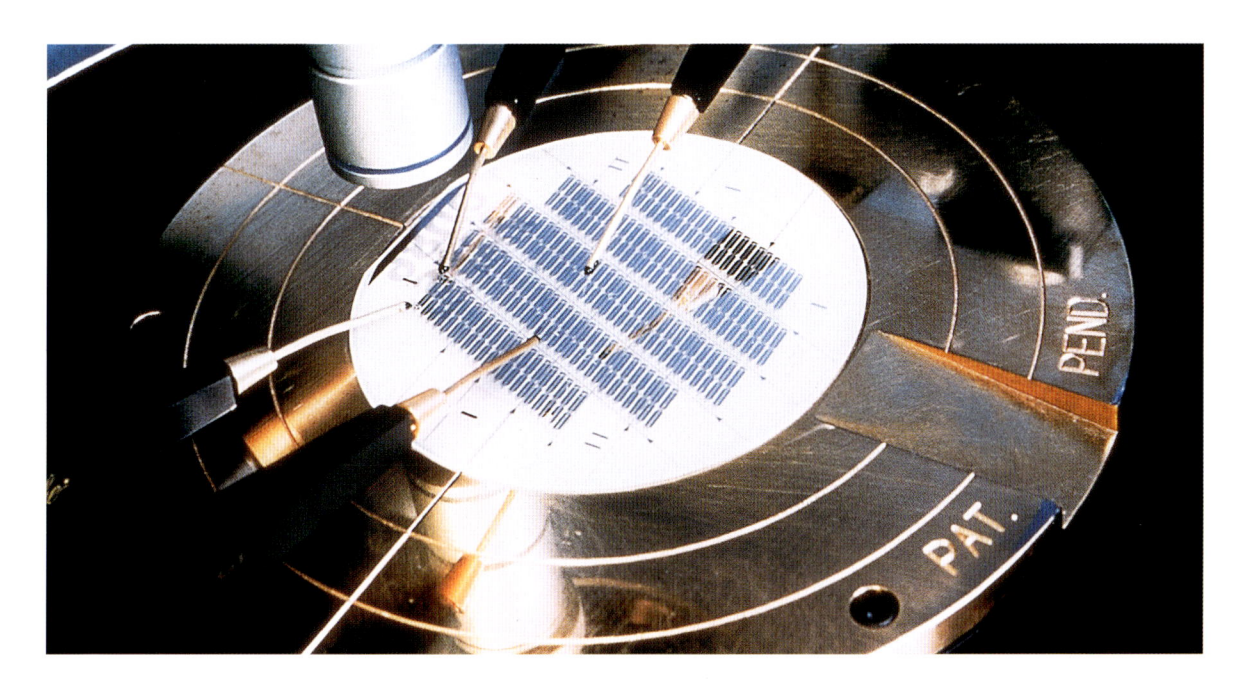

FIGHTING BACK

As the 2002 downturn in the electronics segment persisted, several Dover Technologies companies did not retreat. Vectron International continued its strategic investments to enhance its product line and increase its geographic breadth. Left: A step in the wafer metallization process.

office coped with the increasing difficulty of locating and acquiring attractive stand-alone companies. The corporation had made only two stand-alone acquisitions in 2000: Triton Systems, a producer of off-premise automated teller machines and related software; and OK International, a manufacturer of hand tools and consumable products focused on the circuit board manufacturer workbench. The terrorist attacks of September 11, 2001, had further reduced the available number of companies for sale. Only one of Dover's twelve acquisitions in 2001 was a stand-alone company—Kurz-Kasch, a producer of thermoset plastic-based components and electromagnetic products, founded in 1916 as a switch manufacturer.

Dover was not alone in experiencing a dearth of solid candidates: The third quarter of 2001 recorded the lowest level of mergers and acquisitions among U.S. companies in any quarter during the previous five years. The M&A marketplace remained stuck in the doldrums through 2002, a year in which Dover again acquired only one stand-alone company, Hover-Davis, Inc., a maker of component feeder systems for the electronic assembly automation industry. The company joined the CBAT segment of Dover Technologies.

The four stand-alone acquisitions executed from 2000 through 2002 were companies that offered solid growth prospects but did not perfectly square with Dover's revised platform strategy. "We didn't want to lose the ability to acquire neat, modest-sized businesses that had good growth potential but might not rise to platform status or size," Tyre explains.

DOVER CORPORATION LAUNCHING PAD

AUTONOMY: ENERGIZING BUSINESS

In the wake of the two oil embargoes of the 1970s, when the scarcity of foreign oil caused a sharp increase in domestic petroleum production, Dover's W. C. Norris division—the world's largest sucker rod manufacturer and marketer—was the corporation's standout performer. The company earned as much as 40 percent of the corporation's overall income in the early 1980s, a war chest Dover later plundered for numerous acquisitions. But, in the topsy-turvy oil equipment market, Norris's fortunes repeatedly ebbed and flowed. In 1980, the corporation projected "no end to this boom in sucker rod demand." Two years later, the end had come. Norris's star had fallen precipitously; the company's spanking new plant, able to produce 125,000 feet of sucker rods a year, was mired by a market demand for less than 80 million feet and produced less than 48 million feet.

Tom Reece, Norris's president at that time, reorganized the suddenly ailing organization into five separate divisions, each with its own president. He reduced employment, downsized facilities, cut capital expenses, and otherwise held tight for the market's rebound. In 1986, Norris lost money for the last time in its history thus far, but business nevertheless ambled along sluggishly, the oil equipment market failing to regain its former momentum.

In 1991, the five Norris divisions were consolidated into three: Norris, which predominantly makes sucker rods; Norriseal Controls, which makes butterfly valves; and Alberta Oil Tool, which manufactures sucker rods, fittings, valves, and controls. "We resized and restructured the business, becoming a much leaner company," says Jim Mitchell, president of Norris at the time. "We cut our inventory turns and reduced our supplier relationships while improving our customer service. Dover, meanwhile, invested millions in new machinery for us, such as automatic forging equipment, giving us the opportunity to enhance our manufacturing processes and overall efficiency. We became more differentiated in the marketplace, helping us to widen our lead on the competition."

But the oil equipment market in the late 1990s continued to rise and fall with the price of petroleum. In 1998, the market again collapsed, and profits at the three petroleum equipment companies declined by more than 50 percent. The heyday of contributing 40 percent of Dover's income during the oil boom of the early 1980s seemed a thing of the distant past; at the end of 1998, the three companies together had produced less than 2 percent of Dover's operating profits. Still, Reece, by then CEO and chairman of Dover and well-versed in the cyclicality of the boom-bust market, remained optimistic: "Things change, and will change again," he said.

Reece was right. In 1999, market demand for equipment used to produce oil and gas increased sharply, and the three companies, reorganized as Dover's Petroleum Equipment Group, scrambled to keep up with the steady flow of orders. Two years later, the three companies together recorded their most profitable year since the early 1980s, due tribute to the various cost-cutting initiatives and investments in capacity made by Dover over the years.

Today, the renamed Energy Products Group within Dover Resources is among Dover's largest platform companies. In addition to the original three (Norris, AOT, and Norriseal), EPG includes two former stand-alone companies (Quartzdyne, a maker of quartz-based pressure transducers, and Ferguson-Beauregard, a maker of plunger lift and well automation systems) as well as Dover's largest add-on acquisition in 2004 (U.S. Synthetic, a manufacturer of polycrystalline diamond cutters used in drill bits for oil and gas exploration).

ENERGIZING STRATEGY

Dover's Energy Products Group is a platform organization bringing together several operating companies in the petroleum equipment market, among them Alberta Oil Tool, an Edmonton, Alberta–based maker of sucker rods, fittings, valves, and other products, above. It was acquired in 1962.

On the bright side, by 2002 several operating companies had evolved into well-built platforms, including DEK Printing, Vectron, Imaje, Everett Charles Technologies, Universal Instruments, Heil Environmental, Heil Trailer International, Rotary Lift, DE-STA-CO Industries, Sargent Controls, Performance Motorsports, Inc., Hill PHOENIX, OPW Fueling Components, and OPW Fluid Transfer, among others. Dover had invested its free-cash-flow profitably into dozens of strategic acquisitions undertaken by these companies to enhance their technology or product lines, boost market share, or expand into related fields.

Take the case of Tulsa Winch, which Dover had acquired in 1996. Through a series of well-conceived add-on acquisitions from 1999 through 2001, this leading maker of winches for the petroleum and construction industries significantly expanded its product offerings, revenues, and profitability. The company's acquisitions included DP Winch, the world leader in winches for military applications and a leader in winches for the towing and recovery industry; Pullmaster, a Canadian company and market leader in winches for the logging, marine, and fishing industries; and Greer, a California company making electronic load-monitoring equipment for the mobile crane industry. Today, Tulsa Winch is the market leader in the North American industrial winch market and is poised for major international expansion.

HAPPY TOGETHER

The union of Hill Refrigeration and Phoenix Refrigeration Systems in 1994 was a synergistic combination. Since acquisition and consolidation had worked so well in the formation of Hill PHOENIX, the operating company continued to make acquisitions from 1997 to 2004.

DOVER CORPORATION LAUNCHING PAD

SOLID PLATFORM

Tulsa Winch demonstrates Dover's platform-building strategy at work, above, with the construction of a military winch by subsidiary DP Winch. With Dover capital behind it, the company also acquired PullMaster and Greer Company, enhancing its product line and technology.

Other platforms were built not just through add-on acquisitions. Some were bolted together by combining different Dover operating companies that, from a marketing standpoint, made sound business sense to unite. For example, DI Foodservice Companies was built in 2000 by uniting Groen, Randell, and Avtec from an operations perspective to address market and distribution advantages. Comparable reasons were behind the formation of SEC Companies, composed of Dover's specialty electronics companies, such as Vectron and Novacap. Some companies within operating companies also migrated over to other operating companies to reinforce their platforms—for example, when Airtomic joined Sargent Controls & Aerospace in 2001.

The market downturn in 2001 and 2002 inevitably spawned corporate divestitures—and Dover was no exception. From 2002 to 2004 Dover sold fourteen businesses; all were small and several were "related diversification" add-ons. "These were companies whose growth had faltered and, in our judgment, would not meet our traditional performance metrics for some time, if ever again," Tyre explains. "The companies faced strategic challenges from larger businesses and, consequently, long-term troubles. If a larger company comes along and makes an offer to buy a company with this set of problems, and the offer is clearly superior, we will entertain it."

To gain deeper insight into the financial health of Dover companies, Tyre embarked upon a retrospec-

INNOVATION: TULSA WINCH'S RN100P

Tulsa Winch Group continues to lead the marketplace in innovative winch designs, raising the bar with its unique RN100P Planetary Winch. The RN100P offers a two-speed hydraulic motor with shift-on-the-fly capability; single, externally mounted air shift cylinder; integral spring-applied, hydraulically released multiple disk brake with hydraulic brake valve and over-running clutch; an air-operated band brake; and a drum with deep cast cable pocket and retention ridges. All TWG companies began as privately held entities with the origination of Tulsa Winch dating back to 1929. TWG represents an integrated group of internationally recognized industry leaders specializing in the manufacture of standard and engineered winch, gearbox, and load information systems for the utility, crane, construction, truck equipment, marine, fishing, construction, logging, drilling, mining, and dredging markets.

---

tive analysis of every acquisition executed by Dover from 1985 through 2000—135 companies in all. His chief objective was to determine whether the economic metrics and other criteria Dover observed when making acquisitions had stood the test of time. The study revealed "we weren't as good as we thought we were, in terms of financial results," Tyre concedes.

The traditional process for examining the economic viability of acquisitions at Dover was to examine their internal rate of return. "We gave the board of directors two economic metrics: a static one—how much we were going to pay for the company, including any debt assumed divided by the EBITA (earnings before interest, taxes, and amortization)—and a speculative one—the internal rate of return-on-purchase-price based on a forecast of after-tax cash flows going out ten years."

Tyre analyzed the 135 acquisitions by comparing actual versus originally forecast internal rates of return. In cases in which Dover had owned a company for fewer than ten years, he asked the respective company presidents and chief financial officers to provide a new forecast based on current projections. He then evaluated this data, thinking he would learn that Dover had reaped an approximate 15 percent return on the investment in each of these companies. "Instead, I learned we were in the low double digits," he says. "We were shooting for 15 percent and ended up with more like 12 percent. Needless to say, this was a surprise because a lot of these companies were really first rate. But some of them had a bad first couple of years, which killed their internal rate of return."

Although he says he conducted a "harsh analysis," Tyre

FLUID TRANSITION

Acquired by Dover in 1994, Midland Manufacturing today is part of OPW Fluid Transfer Group. Midland manufactures valves, such as pressure release valves, left, and level measurement devices that are easy and economical to operate, as well as reliable.

DOVER CORPORATION   LAUNCHING PAD

TAKING STOCK

On November 7, 2002, as part of its annual membership dues in the New York Stock Exchange, Dover—an NYSE-listed corporation since 1956—was privileged to take part in the closing bell ceremony. Above: The Dover board and management on the Stock Exchange floor. Right: The gavel Tom Reece used to summon the close.

believes, economically, it was the most appropriate one. "As I looked at individual stand-alone acquisitions, the ones that didn't do well were the ones where we had violated our own criteria, such as a situation where the company's owner did not manage it post-acquisition or the company was in a very narrow niche and was not a growth platform," he explains. "So the lesson for stand-alone acquisitions was to simply be more disciplined and be sure to follow our golden rules. The add-on acquisitions were another story."

Although the average internal rate of return on investment for the add-on acquisitions compared favorably to the average rate of the stand-alone acquisitions, Tyre comments that some add-ons were "home runs and others were strikeouts"—that is, they had internal rates of return of more than 20 percent and less than 5 percent, respectively. Digging more deeply into the data, he mined some interesting causes for the disparity and then reported his findings to Reece, the subsidiary CEOs, and other senior executives at an executive management meeting. The site of the meeting was a log cabin in Wisconsin; the meeting is part of Dover lore today, referred to as the infamous "heat retreat," an allusion to the sweltering heat wave that had overcome the region as well as to the searing subject matter under review.

"What we had discovered was that a good company can get in trouble pretty quickly if it makes a bad acquisition," Tyre elaborates. "But many company presidents had felt if they didn't do an add-on acquisition they weren't a manly company president. Others would go pretty far down the road of negotiating an acquisition to the point where it was hard to say, 'no.' They had put their egos on the line, and it was tough to pull back. Some even said they wanted to stop the process, but they couldn't. Meanwhile, the subsidiary CEOs were out making stand-alone acquisitions and, with increasingly large portfolios, couldn't exercise the degree of oversight that, in hindsight, they should have. But things were going well: We were breaking records, and we felt if it wasn't broken, there was nothing to fix."

The meeting culminated in the formation of new threshold requirements for undertaking add-on acquisitions, a formal set of rules and principles that were distributed to the operating company presidents at their respective subsidiary presidents' meetings. Presenting the directive to the company presidents was a delicate matter, given the corporation's historic paradigm of decentralized operations and management autonomy. "We wanted company presidents to continue to make decisions they believed were in the best interests of their organizations; but, when it came to add-on acquisitions, we wanted to ensure they followed more specific guidelines," Reece explains. "This is just good, normal business practice, a road map of due diligence that any corporation would follow. We have more properly defined and quantified what synergy means and explicitly require it as a condition of acquisition; otherwise, the acquisition is not strategic. We also strongly emphasize the need for a well-executed program to integrate a new company into the buyer's organization, another critical ingredient of success."

The threshold requirements included many of the same principles that had historically governed Dover acquisitions, such as an acquisition candidate having a successful track record and the operating company management having the ability to take on the additional strategic challenge of acquiring and managing other companies. The process has been refined, however. Presidents now have to demonstrate an acquisition candidate's strategic fit at the earliest date possible, explicating the synergies, risks, integration challenges, and expected associated costs. They also must provide Dover's corporate office with regular assessments of their due diligence. Finally, the bar has been raised on a target company's financial metrics. "Since synergy is a must for add-on acquisitions, the business should be more valuable to us than to the current owners," Tyre argues. "Consequently, we're looking for an internal rate of return above 15 percent and closer to 20 percent. We also now require, post-acquisition, frequent reporting on results versus the internal rate of return model and the key assumptions therein, as well as on the integration effort."

There was another adjustment to Dover's time-honored acquisition criteria. Although the corporation traditionally eschewed buying a company in a turn-around situation, it loosened its standards to allow the purchase

DOVER CORPORATION LAUNCHING PAD

NEW IN LINE

Ron Hoffman's path to Dover CEO in January 2005 began when he bought Tulsa Winch and successfully refocused the ailing company. An individual with vision and strong work ethics, he served as CEO of Dover Resources before heading Dover.

of so-called "Fallen Eagles," companies with great brand names and a history of Dover-valued results that were poorly managed and had fallen upon hard times. "This category is of interest if we believe the new management has successfully begun a turn-around program that is sustainable, one that will return the company to its past glory," Reece comments.

Modifications other than the revamped acquisition measures also were afoot. The corporation's traditional stance against certain centralized processes was relaxed, without obviating the independence and autonomy at the heart of the Dover Philosophy. "There are some things that, as a corporation, we have to do centrally, such as quarterly earnings reports, conference calls with analysts, and so on," Reece explains. "There are other things we do centrally because fundamentally it makes sense to do them, such as the administration of the corporation's 401K plan. But we do this differently than other corporations in that we don't mandate joining; it's left up to the companies to make the decision to participate or not."

The same voluntary provision applied to Dover's corporate health care plan. The corporation believed it could offer operating companies a better price on their 401K and health care plans because of the financial benefit of aggregating many employees under one umbrella. "When the operating companies save money, Dover saves money," Reece says. "But, if they would rather stay with their current plans, it's completely up to them." As of 2004, all but one Dover operating company had joined the 401K plan, and 40 percent of Dover's workforce participated in the health care plan.

The 401K and health care plans were not the only examples of more centralized activities. Several operating companies had joined together in forming so-called "purchasing groups," negotiating steel or fasteners as a single entity to reap volume-based discounts, rebates, and other cost savings. Such practices would not have been encouraged under the old regime. But ment here whose job it is to interact with companies when it comes to their IT initiatives, particularly in the enterprise management and supply-chain management areas," he explains. "He is a resource to the companies, a consultant who does not have the authority to tell them what to do but hopefully employs the Socratic method of asking questions to urge them in the right direction. We also have regular meetings to share best practices on things like state-of-the-art design, lean manufacturing, engineering, and so on. If the companies need us to organize a council on manufacturing, engineering,

---

"OUR CULTURE OF EXTENDING AUTONOMY TO EACH OPERATING COMPANY AND PROVIDING A CLIMATE WHERE PRESIDENTS RUN THEIR COMPANIES AS IF THEY OWN THEM WILL ALWAYS BE THE HALLMARK OF DOVER."

— Ron Hoffman, Dover Corporation CEO (2005–present)

Reece was open to those shared activities as long as they originated with the operating companies. "If there are internal impetuses to do something that the companies believe will reap cost efficiencies, I have no problem with them," he confirms. "Now, this is quite a bit different from me going out and hiring a vice president of procurement who would mandate centralized purchasing across the organization. The push-back from the companies on that would be unbelievable. They would throw me out."

Centralized to Reece was not necessarily a bad word. "We have a vice president of information manage- or marketing, we're here to organize it. But these are typically bottom-up efforts. The companies own these programs, not Dover corporate."

Another change also was underway, albeit a more subtle one. Reece often had stated that the most important job at Dover was that of the operating company president. "Really, what makes Dover work is the company presidents," he insists. Beginning with the "Tilt Toward Growth" in the mid-1990s, Reece had increased the responsibility and accountability of presidents while rewarding them more for superior growth. Consequently, many companies had grown substantially in size and

DOVER CORPORATION LAUNCHING PAD

PASSING THE "TORCH"
It is a Dover tradition—dating to the Durham-to-Sutton handoff—for the retiring CEO to hand over this object to his successor. Here, Tom Reece passes the object affectionately known as "the headdress" to Ron Hoffman.

stature. Reece now wanted to tie these companies back to Dover Corporation insofar as how the public and their customers identified them.

For the first time since the formation of the subsidiaries, individual operating companies were presented as part of Dover Corporation. For example, Rotary Lift, which formerly advertised itself as "Rotary Lift, A Dover Industries Company," presented itself as of 2002 as "Rotary Lift, A Dover Company." "Once it became apparent that we were not going to be spinning off the subsidiaries, it became somewhat more important to re-create the Dover identity," Reece explains.

As 2002 turned into 2003, Reece mulled over other thoughts. He had spent nearly ten years at the helm and "was becoming pretty tired of the recession and the grind," he says. He also neared the age at which most people begin to think earnestly about their retirements. "Every job I ever had at Dover, I've assumed that one of my principal responsibilities was to provide for my own succession," he says. "It went with the territory and was true when I came into this job. Right from day one, I started thinking about who might be in a position, given their broad experience base, to be a logical successor. Just as fit and compatibility are important to the success of our acquisition program, so are fit and compatibility—and continuity—in the CEO position."

As the years passed, various factors, including timing and a potential successor's age, came into play. Many potential candidates were relatively young and had limited corporate experience other than as an operating company president. "I felt that a legitimate candidate should have some successful oversight experience before moving to New York as a possible successor," Reece says. Of the four subsidiary CEOs fitting that profile, three were older than Reece; and the youngest, Rudy Herrmann, had advised the board in February 2001 that he planned to leave the company by the end of the year. Herrmann was succeeded by Ron Hoffman in January 2002. "Ron had taken to the oversight job as executive vice president at Dover Resources very, very effectively, which made him a top candidate to become Dover CEO," Reece comments. "But he needed to experience running his own show at the subsidiary level."

Within months, it was apparent that Hoffman was strong CEO material. "Ron performed superbly and established his credentials," says Reece. "He was very well received by the Dover Resources presidents and by his peer subsidiary CEOs." It was increasingly clear to Reece

INNOVATION: PDQ'S LASERWASH 4000

PDQ Manufacturing created the new benchmark in vehicle wash systems with the groundbreaking LaserWash 4000 series in 1990. The LaserWash 4000, which received the gold award as the most technologically innovative equipment at the 2001 Equip'Auto Exposition in Paris, pioneered the process of electronically measuring each vehicle and providing optimum cleaning distance. PDQ's powerful touch-free technology sweeps consistently across each vehicle, covering even those hard-to-reach surfaces others may miss. The system also allows owners to multi-task: Operators can track money, produce management reports, diagnose problems, and even program lucrative special services and wash cycles to address seasonal wash conditions. PDQ recently introduced the LaserWash G5 S-Series—the new technology standard in the industry—which provides higher throughput while using fewer resources, such as electricity, water, and chemicals.

---

who would succeed him. Effective July 1, 2003, Dover's board of directors appointed Hoffman president and chief operating officer, with the intention that he would succeed Reece no later than the end of 2004. "There was no question about Ron's integrity or his enthusiasm for the Dover culture," Reece insists. "He'll stay focused on the mission and preserve the culture. Like the rest of us here, he believes that operating autonomy, where decisions are made close to the customer, produces the best long-term results."

Reece still had more than a year left in his term, and there was much work to be done. Fortunately, Dover's 2003 financial results offered some respite from the dour conditions of 2001 and 2002. Thanks to revived industrial and technology markets and the aggregate impact of Dover companies "doing the right things," the corporation generated the second highest sales and third highest net earnings per share in its history. The positive news was underscored by a dramatic rebound at Dover Technologies and an especially robust performance by Dover Resources.

Still, the biggest news of 2003 was the $326 million purchase of Warn Industries, Dover's largest-ever acquisition. Oregon-based Warn is the world's most recognized brand in winches and wheel hubs for off-road vehicles, as well as the market leader in truck winches and four-wheel-drive hubs. The company was founded in 1948 by Arthur Warn, the inventor of the wheel-end disconnect hub lock that converted thousands of surplus military Jeeps

TOOLING UP

OK International products run the gamut, from soldering/desoldering stations, left, to optical inspection equipment, bench-top fume extraction systems, fluid-dispensing solutions, and air purification solutions.

DOVER CORPORATION   LAUNCHING PAD

JEEP GENIUS

In 1948, Arthur Warn (standing), a Willy's Jeep dealer in Southpark, Washington, invented the LockOmatic Hub—a device that turned a four-wheel drive, off-road vehicle into a street-maneuverable two-wheel drive. Dover acquired WARN Industries in 2003.

INNOVATION: WARN'S IWE TECHNOLOGY

Warn Industries founder Arthur Warn's extraordinary invention of the wheel-locking hub serves as the foundation for constant innovation at Warn today, such as the company's Integrated Wheel-End (IWE) technology, which offers a simple solution to the fuel consumption problem posed by four-wheel-drive systems. Ford Motor Company wanted to increase the fuel efficiency of the power train on its market-leading F-150 4 x 4 line of pickup trucks, which were challenged by previous four-wheel-drive to two-wheel-drive conversion devices that created energy-sapping drag. Warn responded with an innovative torque management solution that virtually eliminates drag in 2WD. Highly engineered, robust disconnect components combine to engage or disengage the wheel ends whenever the transfer case is shifted, either automatically or manually. The result is four-wheel drive only when needed, preserving fuel and maximizing driver convenience.

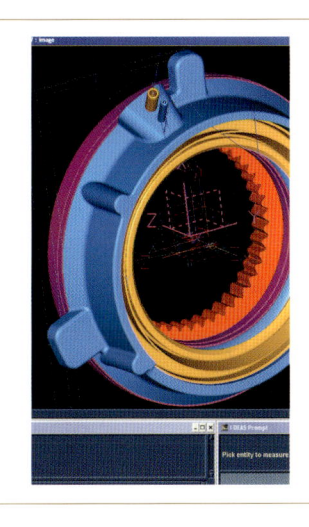

from World War II into useful, on-road vehicles. Ingenuity was in Warn's blood, and in 1959 his company unveiled the first recreational vehicle electric winch. In 1988, as the All-Terrain Vehicle market was emerging, Warn also patented the industry's first ATV self-recovery winch. "Warn has a reputation for taking mechanical concepts and finding markets for them," says Ron Hoffman, whose previous experience at Tulsa Winch was a factor in acquiring the company.

"When we bought Warn," Hoffman notes, "it had just introduced its 'WARN Works' line of smaller, portable do-it-yourself-type winches for projects like pulling a boat out of water or hauling a few bales of hay on a farm. This was a radical concept in the marketplace that didn't exist previously. The winches are inexpensive, roughly $150 each, and we thought the new line might do $3 million in business annually. It did three times that."

Warn flawlessly illustrates the type of company Dover pursues as a platform for growth. "Warn fits the bill perfectly," says Tyre. "It has global breadth, management depth, and a strong channel to market. It boasts a great brand name and intellectual property plus product innovation capability to drive significant future growth. These are all qualities that last. . . . If Dover could do one Warn acquisition a year, our shareholders would be tickled pink."

Warn also has the ability to distinguish itself from other potential suppliers to its customer base and sustain that distinctness

WINCH IN A PINCH

Warn Industries' revolutionary breakthrough was the invention in 1960 of the first electric self-recovery winch designed for weekend adventurers, off-road explorers, and hard-working ranchers needing to pull a vehicle out of a ditch or a stump from the earth. Today, Warn offers the 2.5ci winch, left, the latest iteration of Arthur Warn's invention.

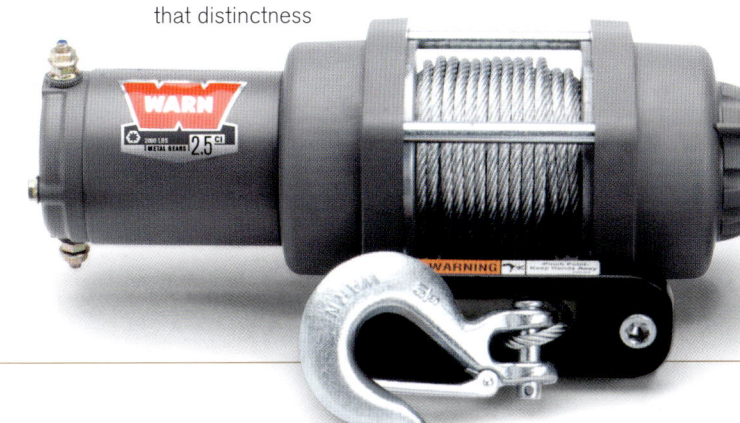

RUGGED RELIABILITY
Warn Industries' extreme duty 9.5ti Thermometric winch—seen here mounted to a Jeep Wrangler—is power personified, providing 9,500 pounds of pulling capacity and a thermal motor feedback sensor, all housed in a massive sealed protective structure.

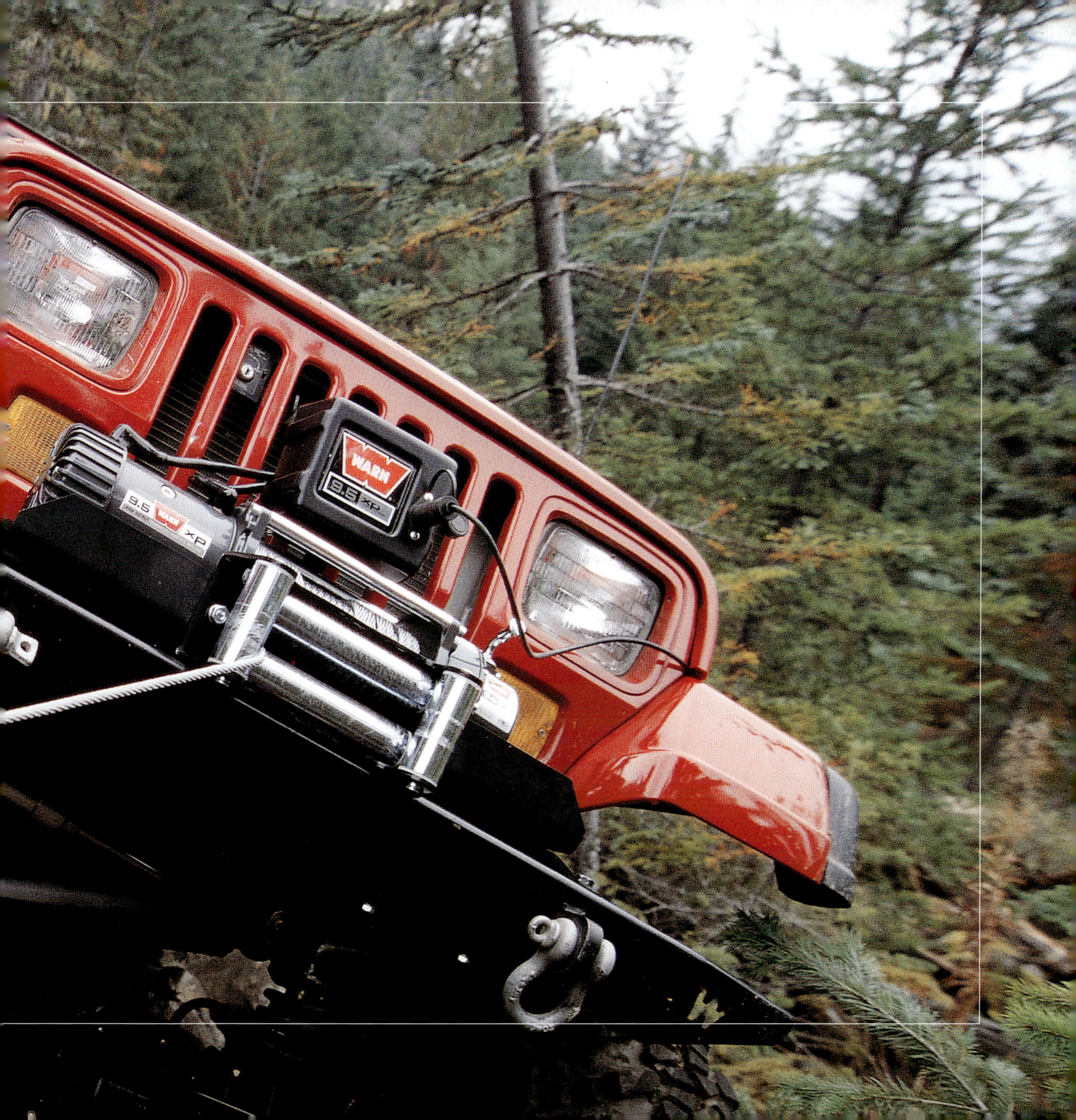
WARN
9.5 XP

DOVER CORPORATION LAUNCHING PAD

over time. Reece calls this trait *defensible differentiation*. "When you have the most knowledge about the customer's needs, the most experience devising solutions to these needs, and a reputation for continually pushing the envelope on these solutions, customers with a problem will come to you first and be willing to pay a premium for your product," Reece explains. "This insight into the customer perpetuates market leadership as long as the

"Years ago, pouring your own castings differentiated you in the marketplace, and we listed numerous foundries in our annual report as a measure of our manufacturing strength," Reece says. "Today, we have one foundry, at Blackmer Pump. As time went by, making your own castings no longer was a core capability. Many Dover companies today buy machined castings, bring them into their facilities, and assemble them with other components

> "IT IS NO LONGER ABOUT SIMPLY HAVING THE GREATEST MANUFACTURING FACILITY. WE MUST HAVE THE GREATEST CUSTOMER INTERACTIONS, THE GREATEST DESIGN CAPABILITIES, AND THE GREATEST INTELLECTUAL PROPERTY SO WE CAN PROTECT WHAT WE DEVELOP."
>
> — Tom Reece, Dover Corporation Chairman of the Board (1999–present)

company continues to invest in its differentiation. To me, that's the definition of a niche company in the twenty-first century."

Knowing its customers and solving their problems in ways that are not easily duplicated by others is what Dover is all about in the global economy, Reece contends. "It is no longer about simply having the greatest manufacturing facility," he declares. "We must have the greatest customer interactions, the greatest design capabilities, and the greatest intellectual property so we can protect what we develop."

Those competencies are far removed from the core characteristics of a Dover company in the past.

into a product that solves a significant customer problem. Look at OPW Fueling Components. They don't cast and machine a single automatic nozzle for dispensing fuel. They found they can go to China and buy machined castings for the nozzles and component parts much less expensively than machining their own castings. This used to be a core competency; no longer. The core competency is solution-providing, putting all the pieces together at the behest of the customer."

Companies that comprehend their core competencies and continually invest in the development of those competencies will be the winners in the global economy, Reece maintains. "A company may think it

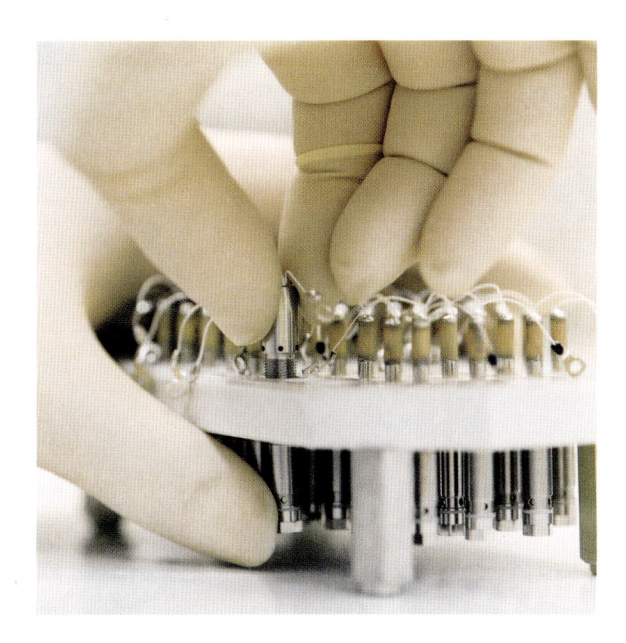

VALUE ADDED

Imaje manufactures the ink, far left, that is used in the printers, near left, they assemble, test, ship, and install for their customers.

is a manufacturer when it really is something else," he explains. "Take the case of Imaje. They don't really make anything other than the ink in their printers because that is the highest value-added part of their product. They execute designs, turn on this incredible network of worldwide suppliers, and then assemble, test, ship, and install their printers. This is the model of the manufacturer of tomorrow."

In his last months as chief executive and preparing for the change-over to a new generation of Dover leaders, Reece was characteristically reflective. Anticipating his continued role as chairman of the board, he expected to add two new tasks to his daily undertakings: He would function as Dover historian and culture co-conservator, apt responsibilities for someone who had begun his career as a Michigan schoolteacher.

Over the course of ten and one-half years as CEO, Reece never averted his focus from the corporation's primary stakeholder, the Dover shareholder. At the end of 1993, Dover's net sales were $1.6 billion, and Reece fully expected they would be double that at the end of 2004. At the same time, the market cap for Dover skyrocketed from approximately $3.35 billion in 1994 to more than $8 billion in 2004 after one of the toughest recessions in memory and the successful divestiture of Dover's largest operating company in 1999.

Thanks to Reece's pronounced emphasis on growth, Dover companies thought and acted more aggressively to expand earnings than had been the case in the past. The corporation financially supported operating companies' add-on acquisitions to a much greater extent, and then tilted its cash compensation program to

DOVER CORPORATION LAUNCHING PAD

LEADERSHIP: THE NEW NAVIGATOR

Dover's fifth CEO, Ron Hoffman, loves the lore. "I enjoy the stories about Tom Sutton being a fighter pilot or George Ohrstrom shooting down the last plane before the end of World War I," he says. "These guys had such amazing lives." Born and reared in a small Oklahoma town, Hoffman says he enjoyed a rather normal youth, shining shoes in a barbershop, playing football on the high school squad, and making friendships that would last a lifetime. His dad was the son of a German immigrant family that came through Ellis Island, and had only an eighth-grade education. His mother died when he was fifteen. Hoffman didn't have any money, so he worked full-time while attending college and receiving both an associate's and bachelor's degree in four years. Partly in jest, he says he yearns for a more extraordinary past to compete with the stories about his colorful forebears. "I wish I was a fighter pilot," he says. "I did once take flying lessons and I do have an aircraft mechanic's license to work on airplanes. That should count for something."

Shortly after receiving a degree in engineering from Oklahoma State, Hoffman took a job in Tulsa as a manufacturing engineer with Vickers Hydraulics, a hydraulic pump and motor company that owned Tulsa Winch, a maker of worm and

---

generously reward real earnings growth. The outcome of these actions was staggering: more than $3 billion invested in more than 165 stand-alone and add-on acquisitions between 1994 and 2004. As he had promised more than a decade before, Reece not only tilted Dover toward growth; he lit the rocket and watched it blast away from the launching pad.

Reece's insatiable curiosity about business management also helped transform Dover into a modern, twenty-first-century corporation. Today, Dover is much more of a global enterprise than it had been in 1994. Dover's on-the-ground international business and exports to overseas markets represent roughly 45 percent of the corporation's business as compared to 30 percent ten years ago. With the acquisition of Imaje in 1995, Reece sent a clear signal that Dover no longer was a North America–centered concern. "It was our first significant international stake in the ground," he says today.

Never able or wanting to shed his schoolteacher genes, Reece could not help but emphasize skills development and "raising the bar" initiatives to improve the depth and breadth of Dover's professional management during his tenure. He recognized early on that pay levels were constraining the organization from drawing the top executive talent that increasingly was needed to effec-

planetary gear winches. He spent the next fifteen years of his life working jobs in every phase of the company until he reached the top as general manager in 1983. Then, in 1985, Vickers asked him to groom Tulsa Winch for sale. When he heard that, Hoffman did something that surprised even himself: Recognizing the hidden value in Tulsa Winch, he said to Vickers' management, "I'd rather buy the company than have you sell it to someone else."

It was a defining moment for Ron Hoffman. He put every ounce of energy he had into rounding up the money to buy Tulsa Winch, going from bank to bank, ready to hock his house, cars, and retirement account. After finding a financial backer, Hoffman bought the company he loved. New products and a focus on serving the original equipment manufacturing market helped the previously ailing company turn a corner.

His extraordinary success in turning around Tulsa Winch attracted Dover Corporation, which bought the company in 1996 despite its small size. Within a short time, Hoffman completed several key acquisitions to roll up the domestic industrial winch industry before moving to Dover Resources, becoming its executive vice president and, later, CEO. He became Dover's fifth chief executive in January 2005. "I had no vision, thoughts, desires, or plans to end up in the corner office at Dover's headquarters," Hoffman says. "I truly am a very lucky person that worked hard, got some breaks along the way, and always believed somehow, someway, things would work out. It has been a helluva ride from growing up in a small house under the water tower in Collinsville, Oklahoma, to an office on Park Avenue in New York City." Add it to the lore.

TULSA TORNADO

After selling Tulsa Winch to Dover in 1996, Ron Hoffman stayed on as president, but was soon named the executive vice president of Dover Resources, then CEO of Dover Resources, and eventually of Dover Corporation.

tively run Dover's ever-larger, geographically dispersed platform companies. "Good enough" was no longer good enough. "We needed to get and retain the best talent we could find, while helping our internal talent to enhance their skill levels," he says.

"There was some resistance at the subsidiaries to the higher pay levels at first, but it dissipated with the realization that we could attract significantly stronger talent with the increased compensation levels. Not only have we sent a lot of promising young managers for MBA training; we have, in fact, attracted some good young talent because they know that, if they perform, we will support and pay for their advanced training,"

Reece says. "When Ron Hoffman gets ready to find his successor, I firmly believe that there will be a significantly larger pool of talent from which to select."

Reece has good feelings about Dover's performance during the boom and bust years, such as the difficult period from 2001 to 2002. In the face of significantly reduced earnings results, Reece stood firm on his pledge to assist companies to do the right things, supporting and encouraging company presidents to invest in the long-term future of their businesses. Likewise, he commends the supportiveness of Dover's independent, knowledgeable board, which has consistently promoted the Dover culture, most recently backing management's decision

DOVER CORPORATION   LAUNCHING PAD

to invest in new product development by the operating companies. "Making such a significant financial commitment requires a long-term view and good understanding by a board of directors," Reece says. "I am grateful we stayed the course. The benefits are already evident as the economy recovers and will be even more evident in the years to come."

Candid and outspoken, Reece also concedes some disappointments as CEO. Although he is pleased with the corporation's acquisition program, he says some companies in the 1998–2000 time frame should not have been purchased. "We didn't properly understand the different requirements for being successful with add-on acquisitions, and I didn't properly realize to what extent 'doing a deal' had become the equivalent of the modern-day gunfighter 'putting a notch in their gun' for our company presidents," he says. "We should have been more prepared to 'just say no' in a few cases. Our failure to do that left too many messes for Ron and his team to clean up early in his tenure as chief operating officer, with some overhang as he became CEO. Hopefully the 'lessons learned' from our earnest attempts to thoroughly assess our results will help Dover avoid repeating our mistakes as the environment for acquisitions heats up in the future."

Beginning with his days of answering the phones and mailing brochures at Ronningen-Petter, Tom Reece spent his entire business career with Dover Corporation. He was infused with the Dover culture. It permeates his being in the same way it affected Fred Durham, Tom Sutton, and Gary Roubos. Perhaps Reece's singular achievement was the fact that Dover's unique and powerful culture was as strong at the end of his tenure as it had ever been. "There are a lot of people who didn't believe the Dover Philosophy could continue to work in an organization of this size and breadth," Reece asserts. "It does, and it will continue to in the future as long as everyone in top management and on the board keeps the right ego and believes in the intrinsic goodness of people."

The foundations for the Dover culture are "the highest standards of honesty, integrity, and two-way trust," Reece says, "the best of human psychology at work." Awhile back, he coined the slogan, "Be happy, but never satisfied," as the theme for one of Dover's annual presidents' meetings. "I guess that phrase pretty much summed up my feelings as I came to the end of my active role as CEO, and it pretty much sums up my career at Dover," he confides. "I've been and am extremely happy. But I've not been, and never will be, satisfied."

When Reece devised his concept of defensible differentiation in 2004, it was Ron Hoffman who delivered the message to Dover companies, having inherited the day-to-day dealings as the corporation's chief operating officer. Warm, modest, and self-effacing, Hoffman had moved his family from Tulsa to New York City the previous year. He says he found the Big Apple unfamiliar at first but soon marched to the city's rhythms. Once, while walking to lunch, he bumped into former Dover CEO Tom Sutton, whose office was a few blocks north of Dover headquarters. Sutton, then in his eighties, suffered from poor eyesight but still made the weekly trek from his home in Connecticut to the city. "Once Tom recognized me, he'd launch right into his stories of the Dover lore," says Hoffman. "He'd remind me how great a company it was and is, and always end the conversation with, 'Now, don't f--- it up!' followed by a smile. I was

THE DOVER FAMILY
George Ohrstrom's founding principles of autonomous operating company management matched with management entrepreneurialism, initiative, and responsibility remain the tenets of acquisitions. Far left: The family of Dover operating companies at the time of the corporation's fiftieth anniversary.

DOVER CORPORATION   LAUNCHING PAD

sure that Tom Reece would give me those same stirring comments when I became CEO."

Hoffman had spent much of 2004 rethinking Dover's corporate structure. As in the 1980s, the corporation's girth had become unwieldy from an oversight standpoint. "When the original subsidiaries were created, each was comprised of about six to eight companies with about $300 million in average annual sales," he explains. "By 2004, each subsidiary, due in large part to the successful add-on and platform-acquisition strategies, was comprised of dozens of companies generating an aggregate $1.2 billion to $1.6 billion in sales. Not only were the number of companies and their sizes much bigger; the markets served, geographic locations, and global focus of these companies were far more complex. It was just more challenging to run a subsidiary than when they first were established."

By the summer of the year, Hoffman had devised a solution—the creation of two additional subsidiaries. In October 2004, the new subsidiaries made their debut: Dover Electronics, representing eight companies (the former SEC companies—Vectron, Novacap, K&L Microwave, Dielectric, and Dow Key—as well as Triton, Kurz-Kasch, and Hydro Systems) and Dover Systems, representing five companies (Hill PHOENIX, DI Foodservice, Belvac, SWF, and Tipper Tie). Dover Electronics is headed by Bob Livingston, former president of Vectron, and

Dover Systems is headed by Ralph Coppola, former president of Hill PHOENIX.

Other management changes accompanied the restructuring: Tim Sandker, former president of Civacon and Rotary Lift, succeeded Lew Burns as CEO of Dover Industries; Bill Spurgeon, former president of Sargent Controls & Aerospace, succeeded Jerry Yochum as CEO of Dover Diversified; and Dave Ropp, who had succeeded Hoffman as CEO of Dover Resources in 2003. Only John Pomeroy at Dover Technologies remained from the group of CEOs who had guided the subsidiaries since the mid-1980s.

The new structure was predicated on reducing the number of companies in each subsidiary, but Hoffman also wanted to realign the companies within the subsidiaries to be focused more on macromarkets. Mark Andy, for example, departed from Dover Diversified to join Imaje, its cousin in the marking, printing, and labeling business at Dover Technologies. Similarly, DI Foodservice Companies and Hill PHOENIX, two companies that essentially serve the same macromarket, yet had formerly resided in two separate subsidiaries, were relocated under the umbrella of Dover Systems.

Although Hoffman reworked the corporate structure, he vowed as he became CEO to preserve the Dover Philosophy intact. "Our culture of extending autonomy to each operating company and providing a climate where presidents run their companies as if they own them will always be the hallmark of Dover," he says. "Nurturing companies with defensible differentiation, doing the right things right, and conducting business with the highest standards of integrity will always be the base tenets of Dover. Change in Dover is not taken lightly. We have been very fortunate to have this unique culture that has lasted the past fifty years. As the corporation celebrates its fiftieth anniversary, it is time to provide the foundation for the next chapter in Dover's history."

GOLDEN LEADERSHIP

At the turn of Dover's fiftieth anniversary, the executive management and six subsidiary CEOs gathered for a portrait. Front row from left are Dover Corporation executives Joe Schmidt, Ron Hoffman, Bob Tyre, and Rob Kuhbach. Back row from left are subsidiary CEOs Tim Sandker, Dave Ropp, Bob Livingston, Bill Spurgeon, John Pomeroy, and Ralph Coppola.

DOVER CORPORATION INDEX

A

"A Dover Company" 138
AC Compressor, 103
acquisition criteria
    original, 20, 31, 39, 47, 64, 69, 117
    for platform growth, 116–117
    revised, 82, 118, 135
acquisitions, 67, 76, 84, 87, 118, 145–146, 149
    add-on, 31, 80–82, 98–99, 119, 128
    analysis of, 40, 133–136, 149
    benefits of, 97–98
    criteria and procedures for, 31, 59, 82, 84, 117–119, 135–136
    divestitures of, 76
    as growth platforms, 97, 99, 116–119, 128, 134
    market competition for, 84, 129
    stand-alone, 94, 95, 97, 99, 102, 115, 128, 147
    successes of, 87, 118, 145–146
    synergistic (strategic), 82, 84, 87, 112, 117, 119, 131, 135
    of turnaround companies, 118, 135–136
Advantage, 121
AdVantis platform systems, 75
aerospace industry, 20, 43, 45, 53–54, 70–71, 96, 112
Africa, 25, 35, 41, 65
Airtomic, 71, 132
Alberta Oil Tool, 44, **130**
Algiers, 25
Allan, Hugh, 21, 31, 33, 144, 160
Allen Group, The, 92
Alphasem, 112, **125**
American Expeditionary Services, 20
American Metal Ware, 103
Amsterdam, 119, 120
Apache Junction, Arizona, 66

Apex 2004 Innovation Technology Showcase award, 75
Apple, John, 56
Arbell, 76
Argentina, 93
Asia, 127, 128
Atlanta, Georgia, 25, 86
AT&T Frequency Control Products, 87
automotive industry, 46, 69, 96, 115, 119–120, 125, 127
autonomy. See also Dover Philosophy
    Fred Durham formalizes as a management principle, 24–26
    Gary Roubos refines, 53, 56, 58
    George Ohrstrom establishes as a management principle, 20–21
    Hoffman supports, 139, 151
    Tom Reece restates, 105
    Tom Sutton reinforces principles of, 40–41
Avtec Industries, 132
Axial Lead Sequencer, **49**

B

B-52 bomber, 70
Baltimore, Maryland, 24
Bank of Manhattan Building, 20
Bantam-Pak electronic component testing equipment, **99**
bearings, production of, 44, 49, 76, 120
Bell, Harold, 35
Belvac, 94, 151
Berkshire Hathaway, 105
Bernard Welding Company, 39, 103
best practices, 66, 137
Bethe, Robert "Bob," 24–25, **27**, 30, 39, 52
Binghamton, New York, 113, 122
Blackmer Pump, **28–29**, 31, 47, 75, 84, 90, 144

Blacksburg, Virginia, 24
Boeing Aircraft Company, 112
Boise Cascade, 47, 78
Booz Allen, 91–92
Boug-lès-Valence, France, 96
Boustead, Al, 19, 21
Brant, John, 52, 56
Brazil, 121
Brown, Grant, 86
Bryant, Maggie Ohrstrom, 23
Buffett, Warren, 105
Burns, Lewis, 56, 58–59, 64, 66, 103, 151
Business Week magazine, 48, 91

C

C. Lee Cook Manufacturing Company, 14, **42**, 49, **57**, 69, 71
    manufactures metallic packing, 20, 23, 25
    a "pillar" of Dover Corporation, 22
Cairo, Egypt, 41
Camilla, Georgia, 66
Campbell Elevator, 46
Canada, 131
Caribbean, 66
Carillo Industries, 119–120
Carlisle Corporation, 21–22
Carlisle Tire and Rubber Company, 21
Carr, Chris, **114**
Carr, Tom, 25
Caswell, W. Cameron, 39, 47, 52, 92
Cavanaugh, Tom, 160
CBAT. See circuit board assembly and test industry.
cellular manufacturing, 96–97, 126
centralized management, 32, 53, 137
Chambers, David, 92
Chambon S.A., **119**–120
Chapman, P. W., and Company, 20

Chicago, 20, 38, 58
Chief Automotive Systems, **69**
China, 106, 117, 128, 144
Cincinnati, Ohio, 41, 45
circuit board assembly and test industry, 48–49, 71, 75, 96–98, 102, 110, 121, 126, 128–129
Civacon, 45, **111**, **126**, 151
Cleveland, Ohio, 45
Cold War, 70
Colecto-Pak refuse collection vehicle, **83**
Collinsville, Oklahoma, 147
communications industry, 49, 51, 110, 128
computer industry products, 3, 48–49, 71, 95–96, 98, 106–107, 110, 127
Cook, Charles Lee, 23, 25, 88, **89**
Cook Graphitic Iron, 25
Cook Manley, 57
Coolgenix technology, **87**
Coppola, Ralph, 80, **150**–151, 151
core competency, 48, 98, 144
Credit Lyonnais, 94
Crenlo, 7
Cummins engines, 119
Curtis, Mallet-Prevost, Colt & Mosle, LLP, 160
cyclicality of markets, 27, 44, 94, 122, 130

D

Davenport Machine Tool, 46
Davidson, Bill, 47
Davis, Nigel, 103–104
Dayton, Ohio, 91
DE-STA-CO Industries, 31, 44, 51–52, 84, 88, 131
　develops the toggle clamp, **43**
　and Tom Reece, 91, 113, 122
decentralized management, 24, 26, 27, 41, 135, 136
defense industry, 53, 70, 132
defensible differentiation, 118, 128, 144, 149, 151

DEK Printing Machines, 52, 131
DePere, Wisconsin, 116
Depression, the Great, 19, 21, 33
Detroit, Michigan, 112, 122
DI Foodservice Companies, 132, 151
Dielectric, 151
Dieterich Standard, 47, 49–50, 78, 89, 103
divestiture
　of companies, 40, 71, 105, 110, 111, 117, 145
　as management strategy, 32, 40, 51, 70, 71, 76, 103, 132
　Rob Kubach's experience with, 92
divisional independence, 24, 30, 32
"doing the right things right," 126, 127, 128, 139, 151
"Don't f--- it up!", 36, 51, 149
Dover, Delaware, 22, 160
Dover Canada, 44
Dover CEO succession, 14, 31–32, 34, 44, 46, 49, 79, 138–139
Dover CEOs. *See individual names:* Durham, Fred; Hoffman, Ron; Reece, Tom; Roubos, Gary; Schwenk, Otto; Sutton, Tom.
Dover Components, 56
Dover Corporation
　annual reports, **31**, 75–76, 97, **105**, 112
　board of directors, 21, 30, 64, **80**, 91, 133–134, 147, 149, 160
　executive committee, 30, 31, 39
　executive incentive compensation plans, 67, 69, 81, 84
　executive retreat, 64
　executive summits, 66–67
　formation of, 14–15, 19, 21–22
　a Fortune 500 company, 79
　the "four pillars" of, 22
　investment in own Dover stock, 69, 71, 75, 76, 77, 105

　listed on the New York Stock Exchange, 23, 24
　public offering, 94
　shareholders, 64, 84, 103, 105, 145
Dover Corporation earnings and profits
　in 2000-2005, 111, 122–123, 128, 139, 145, 151
　in the 1960s, 32, 34
　in the 1970s, 47, 49, 51
　in the 1980s, 51, 59, 74
　in the 1990s, 75, 76, 78, 96, 106–107, 145
Dover Corporation headquarters
　centralization of responsibilities at, 27, 136–137
　decentralization of responsibilities at, 27, 41
　in Louisville, Kentucky, 23
　in New York, 37, 39, 74, **77**
　oversight responsibilities, 25, 27, 53, 67
　staffing of, 25, 77
　in Washington D.C., 24
Dover culture, 64, **89**, 111, 149
　cultivated, 67
　and the entrepreneurial spirit, 91, **118**, 139, 147, 151 (*See also* Dover Philosophy)
　formulated, **26**
　and "lean" management, 77, 79
Dover Diversified, 71, 94, 111, 115, 151
　earnings, 110, 123
　formation of, 56, 58, 65, 70
Dover divisions, 31, 40
　autonomous management of, 25, 27, 30, 32, 41, 47, 52, 53
　cope with cyclical nature of markets, 44
　corporate oversight of, 25, 27, 30
　original four, 25
　performance assessment criteria for, 41
　robust earnings and growth among, 49, 53
　Roubos restructures, 56, 58
　presidents, 43
Dover Electronics, 151

DOVER CORPORATION INDEX

Dover Elevator Company, 31, **33**, 44, 47, 65
    earnings and profits, 49, 75
    restructured, 56, 58
Dover Elevator International, 75, 96, 103–104
Dover Elevators, 160
Dover Industries, 9, 56, 94, 110, 151
Dover International, 44
Dover investment bankers, 20–21, 104, 160
Dover Japan, 76
Dover operating companies, 5, 32, 60, 78, 123
    as "A Dover Company," 138
    are market leaders, 7, 69, 86, 97
    autonomous management of, 30, 66, 79, 105, 149, 151
    divestiture of, 145
    and division CEOs, 61, 65
    "Doing the right things right," 126
    Dover CEOs selected from, 65, 88, 91
    ethical leadership of, 89
    formerly divisions, 58
    and globalization, 104, 128
    as growth platforms, 98, 119, 130–131, 132
    improve internal processes, 75, 76
    make acquisitions, 69, 112, 118, 135
    numbers of, 32, 61, 77
    the original four, 22
    pursue aggressive growth strategies, 84, 97
    Reece reaffirms importance of, 105
    Sutton diversifies, 34
    and voluntary centralization, 136–137
Dover operating company presidents, **58**, 66, 67, 69, 118
    should run the company as though they own it, 14, 61, 69
    "the most important job," 121, 137
Dover Philosophy, 66, 81
    Durham formulates, 24, 26
    and Hoffman, 151

    and Reece, 105, 136, 149
    and Roubos, 51
    and Sutton, 34, 40, 59
Dover Resources, 56, 65, 70, 78, 102, 113, 130, 138, 146, 151
    sales and earnings, 110, 123, 139
Dover Sargent, 56
Dover subsidiaries, 65, 67, 150
    acquisitions by, 64, 69, 94, 95, 118
    CEO responsibilities, 61, 64
    CEOs of, **58**, 59, **65**
    divisions restructured as, 56, 58, 70
    executive summits for management of, 66, 67
    productivity, 75, 110
    and recession, 121, 123
    and "Tilt Toward Growth," 81, 84, 91, 111, 150
Dover super-subsidiaries, 56–57
Dover Systems, 56, 151
Dover Technologies, 62, 65, 76, 94, 95, 99, 151
    acquisitions, 102, 118, 128
    formed, 56, 58
    sales and earnings, 71, 74, 95, 106–107, 110, 122–123, 128, 139
Dow Jones stock index, 110
Dow Key, 151
DP Winch, 131, **132**
Dura-Vent, 31, 41
DuraPack refuse collection vehicle, **82**
Durham, Fred, 35, **44**, 58, **88**, **90**
    at C. Lee Cook, 21–23, 25, 89
    as Dover CEO, 14, **22**–23, **24**–25, 31–32, **34**, 36, 41, 77, 89
    ethics and leadership, 23–25, **27**, 30, 31–32, 89
    at Riverview Quail Club, 66, **67**

E

Earles, Bryan, Jr., 44
economic recessions
    of 2001-02, 118, 121, 128, 132
    of the 1970s, 46–47
    of the 1980s, 70–71, 99
    of the 1990s, 75–76, 79, 103, 130
ECT. *See* Everett Charles Technologies.
Edmonton, Canada, 44, 130
electronic equipment, production of, 48–49, 53, 96–97, 106–107, 110, 122, 125–129
electronics industry, 48–49, 51, 53, 122–123, 129
Eliminator electronic component tester, **98**
Ellis Island, 146
Energy Products Group (EPG), 5, 130
Engineered Systems, 45
Ernest Holmes, 46, 71
Europe, 41, 52, 84, 94, 119, 120
Everett Charles Technologies (ECT), 97, **98**, **99**, **110**, 112
    as a platform company, 97, 116, 131

F

Falk, Herman, 93
"Fallen Eagles," 136
Farrell, Dick, 56
Federal Water Service Company, 20
Ferguson-Beauregard, 130
Ford, Henry, 45
Ford Motor Company, 141
Ford River, Michigan, 20
Fordham University Law School, 91
Fortune 500 company, 32, 78, 79, 92
Fortune magazine, 78–79, 81
Forward Manufacturing, 121
France, 119, 120
Frankfurt, Germany, 44

G

Garden City, New York, 91
General Electric, 86
General Host Corporation, 92
Genesis electronic component insertion machine, **48,** 75
Germany, 84, 146
globalization, 81–82, 84, 103, 127–128, 147
Gold Canyon Ranch, 66
Goldman Sachs, 104
Gray, Larry, 79
Great Britain. *See* United Kingdom.
Great Depression, 21, 33
Greer, 131–132
Groen Manufacturing Company, **38**, 39, 76, 103, 132
growth platform, 70, 97, 99, 116–119, 130–132, 141
GSM Component Insertion Equipment, 95–96

H

Hammond & Champness, 46
Harley Davidson, 120
Harvard Business School, 47, 78
Hausfeld, Joseph E., 45
"heat retreat," 134
Heil, Julius, **93**
Heil Company, 60, 93–94, 94, 116
Heil Environmental Industries, Ltd., **60**, 79, 81, **82**, **83**, 93, 94, 121, **127**, 131
Heil Rail Joint Welding Company, 93
Heil Trailer International, **72–73**, 93, 94, 131
Herrmann, Rudy, 88, 138
high-tech industry. *See* computer industry products.
Hill, C. V., 86

Hill PHOENIX, 84, **85**, **87**, **121**, **127**, 151
 a platform company, 116, **131**
Hill Refrigeration, Inc., 84, 85, **86**, 87, 131
Hoffman, Ron, 99, 102, **136**
 background, **146**–147
 as Dover president and COO, **138**, 139, 149
 as Dover CEO, **146**, **150**, 151
 at Dover Resources, 102, 136
 leadership qualities, **136**, 149
 at Tulsa Winch, 77, 99, 102, 136
Hover-Davis, Inc., 129
HTT/Swep, 84
Hunting at Riverview, 84
Huntington Beach, California, 120
hydraulic equipment
 by Heil Environmental Industries, 82
 by Rotary Lift, 19, 31, 33
 by Sargent Controls & Aerospace, 53, 56, 70
 by Texas Hydraulics, 68–69
 by Tulsa Winch, 133
 by Vickers Hydraulics, 146–147
Hydro Hoist Company, 93
Hydro Systems, 103, **104**, 151
HydroGap eductor, **104**

I

IBM, 48
Imaje Group, **96**, 99, 104, 128, 131, **145**, 151
Imaje S.A., 94, 95, 96, **104**, 116
India, 106, 116
internal growth, 30, 70, 75, 127
Italy, 35, 119, 120

J

JE Piston, 119, **120**
Jeep, 141, **142–143**
John Deere, 82
Johnson, Jim, 119

K

Kaizen methods, 75, **127**
Kalamazoo College, 90
Kata, Edward, 52, **53**, 64, 82, 92, 151
K&L Microwave, 52, **53**
Knappco, 45
Kuhbach, Rob, 91, **92**, **150**, 151
Kurz-Kasch, 129, 151

L

Laporte, Cloyd, Jr., 92
LaserWash vehicle system, **139**
Lawson, Floyd "Rudy," 50, 56, 65
"lean" manufacturing
Levine, Ken, 160
Lightning Technology (electronic component placement), **75**
Livingston, Bob, **150**–151
London, 95
long-term growth, 84, 123
Longmont, Colorado, 40
Louisiana Elevator, 46
Louisville, Kentucky, 23, 25, 77
Lucent, 122
Luther & Maelzer, 98–99

DOVER CORPORATION INDEX

M

Madison Avenue, New York, 19
Manhattan, New York, 77
Marathon Equipment, **74**, 75
Mark Andy, Inc., 94, 151
Markpoint Holding, 128
Mars Rover Spacecraft, 87
McKinley, William, (United States president), 93
McKinsey and Company, 39
McNiff, John, 52, **66**, 79, 91
Measurement Systems, 103
Memphis, Tennessee, 30, 33
mergers, 76, 84, 86
Metcal, **128**
Michigan, 59
Midland Manufacturing, 45, **133**
Milwaukee, Wisconsin, 93
Mississippi State Capitol Building, 80
Mitchell, Jim, 130
Model T Ford automobiles, 24, 99
Motorola, Inc., 48

N

National Cash Register, 91
National Coller Company, 121
Netherlands, The, 44, 52
New York City, 18, 19, 20, 40, 66, 93, 94, 112, 149
    Dover corporate offices, 37, 39, 74, 77, 147
New York Society of Security Analysts, 25
New York Stock Exchange, **134**
    Dover Corporation listed on, 23–24
New York University School of Business, 91
Norris, W. C. Company, **5**, 32, 35, 40, 44, 49
    earnings, 46–47, 49, 130
    and economic recessions, 46, 71
    Ohrstrom acquires, 19–20
    a "pillar" of Dover, 22
    and sucker rod plant, 31, **46**, 51
    and Tom Reece as president, 88, 113, 122, 130
Norriseal Controls, 130
Novacap, 132, 151
Nu-Hed Safety pins, 48
Nurad, 76

O

O'Hare Airport, Chicago, 58
Ohio Pattern Works, 45
Ohio Pattern Works and Foundry, 19, 45
Ohrstrom, G. L., & Associates, 19, 21, 33, 39, 40, 45, 160
Ohrstrom, G. L., & Company, 18, 19, 20, 30
Ohrstrom, George L.
    early career, 14–15, 18–21, 23, 160
    founds Dover Corporation, 14, 22
    management philosophy, 14, **20–21**, 77
    as WWI pilot, 15, **16–17**, 20, 146
Ohrstrom, George L., Jr., 20
Ohrstrom, Ricard, 21, 30, 160
oil crises. See economic recessions.
oil industry. See petroleum industry.
OK International, **128**–129, **139**
Oklahoma State University, 146
OPEC, 46
OPW Corporation, **14**, 31, 32, 35, **41**, 44, 69
    and automatic shut-off valve nozzle, 26, **36**, **45**, 47, 144
    and lean manufacturing, 75
OPW Fluid Transfer Group, 126, 131, 133
OPW Fueling Components, 36, 40, 45, 96–**97**, 127, 144
    as a platform company 131
Organization of Petroleum Exporting Companies (OPEC), 46
Ormsby, Tony, 27, 36, 44, 90
Otis Elevator Company, 33

P

Park Avenue, New York City, 39, 74, 77, 147
PDQ, 112, **116**, **139**
Peerless Manufacturing, 19, 40
    a "pillar" of Dover Corporation, 22
Perfect Bore Limited, 119, 120
Performance Motorsports, Inc. (PMI), **119**, **120**, 131
Petroleum Equipment Group, 130
petroleum industry
    equipment for, 19–20, 26, 30, 36, 45, 70
    fluctuations in, 71, 130
Petter, Bill, 47, 88–89, 90–91
Phoenix Refrigeration Systems, 84, **85**, **86**, 94, 131
"pillar" companies of Dover Corporation, 14, 19, 22, 47, 89
PISCES leak-prevention system, 127
pistons, 113–**115**, 119–120
    packing for, 20, 42
platform company. See growth platform.
PME, 76
PMI. See Performance Motorsports, Inc.
Pomeroy, John, 50, 94, 98, 128, **150**–151
    leadership qualities of, 65–66
Princeton University, 91
Prox Inter BV, 119, 120
Pullmaster, 131–132
pumps, 29, 31, 46, 70, 102–104, 127
Purdue University, 50
Python refuse collection vehicle, **60**

156

Q

Quail Club, 66
Quartzdyne, 113, 130
Quartztek, 76

R

Randell Manufacturing, 132
recession. *See* economic recessions.
Reece, Sandy, 112
Reece, Tom, 81, **88**, 95, 98, 115, 118, 119, 126, **134**, 141–143
    accomplishments, 105, 111–112, 145–148, 150
    becomes CEO of Dover, 84
    at DE-STA-CO, 51, 91, 112
    on decentralization, 136–137
    on defensible differentiation, 144–145
    as Dover CEO, 61, 70, 84, 86, 89, **90**, 92, 97, 102, 106, **112**
    as Dover COO, 82
    at Dover Resources, 56, 65, 88
    and Dover restructuring, 58–59
    on economic recessions, 122–123, 128, 130
    issues IPO, 94
    leadership qualities and style of, 61, 65–67, 88–89, 91, 92, 112
    at Norris, 51
    on platform strategy, 116–117
    at Ronningen-Petter, 47, 88, 90, **113**
    selects Ron Hoffman, 99, 138–139
Reggio Emilia, Italy, 120
Retromizer heat transfer equipment, 49
Richards, Gil, 41
Richmond, Virginia, 86
Riverside Quail Club, 66
Rocky Mountain Arsenal, 78
Ronningen-Petter, 39, 47, 88, 90, 113
Root, Helen, 24
Ropp, Dave, **150**–151
Rotary Lift Company, 21, **30**, 40, **47**, 88, 121, 151
    develops auto lift, 19, 127
    develops hydraulic elevator, 19, 31, 33
    earnings, 49, 51, 119
    and lean manufacturing, 75
    a "pillar" of Dover Corporation, 22
    as a platform company, 131
Roubos, Gary, **78**–79, 87, 112
    and Dieterich Standard, 47, 78, 89, 103–105
    as Dover CEO, 49, **50**–53, **64**, 71, **78**–79, **90**, 106
    and Dover restructuring, 56, 58–**60**, 64
    leadership qualities and style, **65**–66
    management practices, 67, 69, 75–76, 118
    selects Tom Reece as successor, 81, 88, 113

S

San Clemente, California, 120
San Dimas, California, 121
Sandker, Tim, 51, **150**
Sargent, Sumner Benedict, 70, 71
Sargent Controls & Aerospace, **54**, 112, 151
    as a platform company, 131–132
    and "quiet valve" technology, **56**, 70
Sargent Industries, 53, 58, **70**, **71**
Schmidt, Joseph, **92**, **150**–151
Schwenk, Otto, 32, 46
SEC (specialty electronics component) industry, 128
semiconductor industry, 48, 98–99, 110, 112
Semiconductor Test Group, **110**
September 11, 2001, 129
Shepard-Warner Elevators., 31
Silicon Valley, California 128
Singer Corporation, 46
Six Sigma, 126
Soltec, 52
Sonic Industries, 112
South Park, Washington, 140
Southern Bell Telephone Company, 25
Spurgeon, Bill, **150**–151
St. Etienne, France, 19
St. Paul, Minnesota, 78
Standard & Poor's, 94, 96
Stanford University, 91–92
Stevensville, Virginia, 24
stock market crash of 1929, 19, 20, 21
Stubbs, Merrill, 30
submarines, 53, 56, 70
sucker rod production, 31, 46, 51, 70, 130
Sudbury, Inc., 92
Suesser, Fred, 39, 43, **66**
super-subsidiary, 56
Sure Seal, 126
Sutton, Thomas, 104, 149
    accomplishments, 34, 39, 59
    as Dover CEO, **34**, **35**, 36, **37**, 46, **50**, **58**, **90**
    management principles and practices, 34, **40**–43, 47, 50–51, 66, 77
    at OPW, **14**, 32, 41
    at Riverview Quail Club, 66–**67**
    selects Gary Roubos as successor, 79
Sweden, 84, 117, 128
SWEP International, **117**
SWF, 151
Switzerland, 112
synergy, 131
    an acquisition criterion, 84, 135
    not an acquisition criterion, 30, 59, 81–82, 84

DOVER CORPORATION ·INDEX

T

TAVCO, 41
Technopak, 84
Texas Hydraulics, **68**–69, 88
Thyssen Elevator, 104
Thyssen Industrie AG, 33, 104
"Tilt Toward Growth," 78, 80, 81, 84, 91, 97, 118
Tinker Products, 41
Tipper Clipper, **52**
Tipper Tie, **52**, 84, 151
Tisdale, Stuart, 46
Tokyo, Japan, 44
Tranter PHE, 49, **84**, 117
Tresise, Victor E., 45
Triton Systems, **122**, **123**, 129, 151
Tucson, Arizona, 70
Tulsa, Oklahoma, 20, 113, 146, 149
Tulsa Winch, 102, 131, **133**, 136, 146–147
    Dover acquires, 77, 99, 147
    as a platform company, 116, 131–**132**
    and the RN100P planetary winch, **133**
Tyre, Robert, 87, 91–**92**
    and acquisition strategy, 118–119, 132–135
    as acquisitions specialist, 82, 94, 117, 122, 129, **150**–151

U

United Kingdom, 20, 52, 119
United States Army Air Corps, 40–41
United States Army Corps of Engineers, 78
United States Federal Reserve, 53
United States Internal Revenue Service, 19
United States Navy, 56, 70
United States Reserve Officer Training Corp, 78
United States Securities and Exchange Commission, 19
Universal Instruments, **3**, **48**–50, **75**, 99, **106**, 112, 113, 118, 131
    earnings, **62**, 71–72, 95, 96, 122
    expands into Asia, 127–128
Universal Instruments and Metal Company, 48
University of Cincinnati, 35
University of Colorado, 78
University of Michigan, 20
    Law School, 92
University of Tulsa, 99
U.S. Synthetic, 130
utility companies, 18–20

V

valves, 19, 31, 45, 56, 70, 126, 130–131, 133
Van Loan, Dave, 98–99
Vectron International, **87**, **94**, **108**, 122, **129**, 131–132, 151
Vectron Laboratories, 87, 94
Vectron Technologies, 87
Vertex Pistons, 119–120
Vestal, New York, 48
Vickers Hydraulics, 99, 146–147
Virginia Polytechnic Institute, 24–25
Vitronics, 102
Vitronics Soltec, 102, **126**

W

W. C. Norris. *See* Norris, W. C.
Wall Street, 19, 21, 39
Walter O'Bannon, 31
Warn, Arthur, 131, **140**, 141
WARN Industries, 139, **140**, **141**, **142–143**
Warsaw, Virginia, 22–23, 58
Washington, D. C., 76, 93
Waukesha Bearings, **44**, 49, 65, **76**
Wave Reflow Selective Soldering Technologies, **126**
Western Michigan University, 88, 90
Westinghouse Elevator Company, 33
Wilden, Jim, 102–103, 113, 115
Wilden Pump and Engineering, **100**, **102**, **103**, 113, 115, 118
Williams College, 91
winches, 99, 131, **132**, **133**, 139, 147
    recreational, 141, **142–143**
Wisconsin, 93, 134
Wiseco Piston, 112–**114**, **115**, 116, 120
Wiseman, Clyde, 113, 115
Wolfe Frostop, 76
World War I, 15, 16, 17, 20, 146
World War II, 41, 70, 141

Y

Yale University, 39, 92
Yochum, Jerry, 65, 70, 71, 86, 115, 119, 151

Boldface indicates pages with images

ABOUT THE AUTHOR

Russ Banham has written more than three thousand articles on business and industry for publications including *Forbes*, *The Economist*, *CFO*, *Financial Times*, *Time*, *U.S. News & World Report*, *Venture*, and *Inc*. The author of eight books, including the best-selling *Rocky Mountain Legend*, the story of the Coors family, and *The Ford Century*, the award-winning centennial history of Ford Motor Company, Banham is a former teaching fellow at the University of Montana, a playwright and professional stage director. He recently directed his play *Ethan Frome*, an adaptation of the Edith Wharton novella, for Book-It Repertory at the Intiman Theatre in Seattle, where he lives with his wife and three children. Banham's television appearances include *The Today Show* and *A&E Biography*.

THE ORIGIN OF THE NAME "DOVER CORPORATION" is cloaked in uncertainty. At least three versions of how the corporation got its name exist, each viable and verifiable. Story Number One has it that Ken Levine, an attorney at Dover's longtime general counsel, Curtis, Mallet-Prevost, Colt & Mosle, LLP, and Tom Cavanaugh, one of George Ohrstrom's partners, were driving when they spied a road sign for the city of Dover, Delaware. Cognizant that G. L. Ohrstrom & Associates was backed by a group of British investors, Levine supposedly commented that "Dover" would be a great name for the corporation because of its English roots. Seems plausible, but then there is Story Number Two, courtesy of Ricard "Ric" Ohrstrom, George's son and a longtime Dover board director. "Father had said he wished the company to have a short, two-syllable, Anglo-Saxon name, one easy to remember," Ric said in a 1988 interview. "I assigned the name 'Warwick' to the project, Warwick having been one of my heroes in English history. Father did not like the name; and, hence, we had to choose another at the last minute." After giving the matter more thought, Ric simply came up with the name "Dover." Hmmm. Story Number Three credits George Ohrstrom with the name. In the book *Dover Elevators*, Hugh Allan, the subsidiary's president, was quoted as saying that Ohrstrom "all of a sudden got the idea from his dealings with his associates in England that 'Dover' would be a good name." Whatever version is true, the name "Dover" unquestionably was a good choice. Indeed, the various individuals involved in the creation of Dover fifty years ago were amazed it was unclaimed by any other corporation.

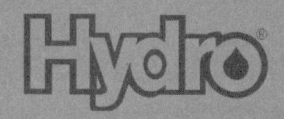

- WARN
- OPW
- Crenlo, LLC
- OPW FLUID TRANSFER GROUP
- WILDEN
- C.Lee Cook
- blackmer
- SWF COMPANIES
- NORRIS
- OK INTERNATIONAL
- SARGENT
- TULSA WINCH
- RPA Process Technologies
- DATAMAX
- DESTACO
- TEXAS HYDRAULICS
- SWEP
- Alphasem
- KOOLANT KOOLERS
- Hydro
- DEK
- Triton
- TRANTER
- HOVER-DAVIS
- DowKey Microwave
- DI FOODSERVICE COMPANIES